PSYCHIC ASSAULTS AND FRIGHTENED CLINICIANS

Other titles in the
Forensic Psychotherapy Monograph Series

Violence: A Public Health Menace and a Public Health Approach
Edited by Sandra L. Bloom

Life within Hidden Walls: Psychotherapy in Prisons
Edited by Jessica Williams Saunders

Forensic Psychotherapy and Psychopathology: Winnicottian Perspectives
Edited by Brett Kahr

Dangerous Patients: A Psychodynamic Approach to Risk Assessment and Management
Edited by Ronald Doctor

Anxiety at 35,000 Feet: An Introduction to Clinical Aerospace Psychology
Robert Bor

The Mind of the Paedophile: Psychoanalytic Perspectives
Edited by Charles W. Socarides

Violent Adolescents: Understanding the Destructive Impulse
Lynn Greenwood

Violence in Children: Understanding and Helping Those Who Harm
Rosemary Campher

Murder: A Psychotherapeutic Investigation
Ronald Doctor

PSYCHIC ASSAULTS AND FRIGHTENED CLINICIANS
Countertransference in Forensic Settings

Edited by
John Gordon and Gabriel Kirtchuk

Foreword by
R.D. Hinshelwood

Forensic Psychotherapy Monograph Series

Series Editor
Brett Kahr

Honorary Consultant
Estela Welldon

Routledge
Taylor & Francis Group
LONDON AND NEW YORK

First published 2008 by Karnac Books Ltd

Published 2019 by Routledge
2 Park Square, Milton Park, Abingdon, Oxon OX14 4RN
52 Vanderbilt Avenue, New York, NY 10017

First issued in hardback 2019

Routledge is an imprint of the Taylor & Francis Group, an informa business

British Library Cataloguing in Publication Data

A C.I.P. for this book is available from the British Library

Edited, designed, and produced by
Florence Production Ltd, Stoodleigh, Devon
www.florenceproduction.co.uk

ISBN 13: 978-0-367-10593-8 (hbk)
ISBN 13: 978–1–85575–562–8 (pbk)

CONTENTS

ACKNOWLEDGEMENTS

The case material in this book has been disguised and comprises composites of many individuals with whom the authors have worked. We are very grateful to the patients and colleagues who have shared the difficult and enlightening emotional experiences on which our clinical thinking is based.

Extensively revised for this publication, a previous version of Chapter Three originally appeared in Group Analysis 38(3): 409–426 and is reprinted by permission of Sage Publications Ltd, © The Group Analytic Society, London, 2005.

We would like to thank Kim Bush, Manager of Photography and Permissions at the Solomon R. Guggenheim Foundation; Jessica Casey, Licensing Executive at the Design and Artists Copyright Society (DACS); and the Kandinsky Estate for their support in arranging for the use of *Circles on Black (Kreise auf Schwartz)*, 1921.

Finally, Brett Kahr, Editor of the Karnac Forensic Psychotherapy Monograph Series, has helped us with panache at every stage. Muchíssimas gracias, Brett.

SERIES FOREWORD

Brett Kahr

Centre for Child Mental Health, London
and
The Winnicott Clinic of Psychotherapy, London

Throughout most of human history, our ancestors have done rather poorly when dealing with acts of violence. To cite but one of many shocking examples, let us perhaps recall a case from 1801, of an English boy aged only 13, who was executed by hanging on the gallows at Tyburn. What was his crime? It seems that he had been condemned to die for having stolen a spoon (Westwick, 1940).

In most cases, our predecessors have either *ignored* murderousness and aggression, as in the case of Graeco-Roman infanticide, which occurred so regularly in the ancient world that it acquired an almost normative status (deMause, 1974; Kahr, 1994); or they have *punished* murderousness and destruction with retaliatory sadism, a form of unconscious identification with the aggressor. Any history of criminology will readily reveal the cruel punishments inflicted upon prisoners throughout the ages, ranging from beatings and stockades, to more severe forms of torture, culminating in eviscerations, beheadings, or lynchings.

Only during the last one hundred years have we begun to develop the capacity to respond more intelligently and more humanely to acts of dangerousness and destruction. Since the advent of psychoanalysis and psychoanalytic psychotherapy, we now have access to a much deeper understanding both of the aetiology of aggressive acts and of their treatment; and nowadays we need no longer ignore criminals or abuse them—instead, we can provide compassion and containment, as well as conduct research that can help to prevent future acts of violence.

The modern discipline of forensic psychotherapy, which can be defined, quite simply, as the use of psychoanalytically orientated "talking therapy" to treat violent, offender patients, stems directly from the work of Sigmund Freud. Almost one hundred years ago, at a meeting of the Vienna Psycho-Analytical Society, held on 6 February 1907, Sigmund Freud anticipated the clarion call of contemporary forensic psychotherapists when he bemoaned the often horrible treatment of mentally ill offenders, in a discussion on the psychology of vagrancy. According to Otto Rank, Freud's secretary at the time, the founder of psychoanalysis expressed his sorrow at the "non-sensical treatment of these people in prisons" (quoted in Nunberg & Federn, 1962, p. 108).

Many of the early psychoanalysts preoccupied themselves with forensic topics. Hanns Sachs, himself a trained lawyer, and Marie Bonaparte, the French princess who wrote about the cruelty of war, each spoke fiercely against capital punishment. Sachs, one of the first members of Freud's secret committee, regarded the death penalty for offenders as an example of group sadism (Moellenhoff, 1966). Bonaparte, who had studied various murderers throughout her career, had actually lobbied politicians in America to free the convicted killer Caryl Chessman, during his sentence on Death Row at the California State Prison in San Quentin, albeit unsuccessfully (Bertin, 1982).

Melanie Klein concluded her first book, the landmark text *Die Psychoanalyse des Kindes* [*The Psycho-Analysis of Children*], with resounding passion about the problem of violence in our culture. Mrs Klein noted that acts of criminality invariably stem from disturbances in childhood, and that if young people could receive access to psychoanalytic treatment at any early age, then much cruelty could be prevented in later years. Klein expressed the hope that: "If every child who shows disturbances that are at all severe were to be analysed in good time, a great number of these people who later end up in prisons or lunatic asylums, or who go completely to pieces, would be saved from such a fate and be able to develop a normal life" (1932, p. 374).

Shortly after the publication of Klein's transformative book, Atwell Westwick, a Judge of the Superior Court of Santa Barbara, California, published a little-known though highly inspiring article, "Criminology and Psychoanalysis" (1940), in the *Psychoanalytic Quarterly*. Westwick may well be the first judge to commit himself in print to the value of psychoanalysis in the study of criminality, arguing that punishment of the forensic patient remains, in fact, a sheer waste of time. With foresight, Judge Westwick queried, "Can we not, in our well nigh hopeless and overwhelming struggle with the problems of delinquency and crime, profit by medical experience with the problems of health and disease? Will we not, eventually, terminate the senseless policy of sitting idly by until misbehavior occurs, often with irreparable damage, then dumping the delinquent into the juvenile court or reformatory and dumping the criminal into prison?" (p. 281). Westwick noted that we should, instead, train judges, probation officers, social workers, as well as teachers and parents, in the precepts of psychoanalysis, in order to arrive at a more sensitive, non-punitive understanding of the nature of criminality. He opined: "When we shall have succeeded in committing society to such a program, when we see it launched definitely upon the venture, as in time it surely will be—then shall we have erected an appropriate memorial to Sigmund Freud" (p. 281).

In more recent years, the field of forensic psychotherapy has become increasingly well constellated. Building upon the pioneering contributions of such psychoanalysts and psychotherapists as Edward Glover, Grace Pailthorpe, Melitta Schmideberg, and more recently Murray Cox, Mervin Glasser, Ismond Rosen, Estela Welldon, and others too numerous to mention, forensic psychotherapy has now become an increasingly formalized discipline that can be dated to the inauguration of the International Association for Forensic Psychotherapy and to the first annual conference, held at St. Bartholomew's Hospital in London in 1991. The profession now boasts a more robust foundation, with training courses developing in the United Kingdom and beyond. Since the inauguration of the Diploma in Forensic Psychotherapy (and subsequently the Diploma in Forensic Psychotherapeutic Studies), under the auspices of the British Postgraduate Medical Federation of the University of London in association with the Portman Clinic, students can now seek further instruction in the psychodynamic treatment of patients who act out in a dangerous and illegal manner.

The volumes in this series of books will aim to provide both practical advice and theoretical stimulation for introductory students and for senior practitioners alike. In the Karnac Books Forensic Psychotherapy Monograph Series, we will endeavour to produce a regular stream of high-quality titles, written by leading members of the profession, who will share their expertise in a concise and practice-orientated fashion. We trust that such a collection of books will help to consolidate the knowledge and experience that we have already acquired and will also provide new directions for the upcoming decades of the new century. In this way, we shall hope to plant the seeds for a more rigorous, sturdy, and wide-reaching profession of forensic psychotherapy.

As the new millennium begins to unfold, we now have an opportunity for psychotherapeutically orientated forensic mental health professionals to work in close conjunction with child psychologists and with infant mental health specialists so that the problems of violence can be tackled both preventatively and retrospectively. With the growth of the field of forensic psychotherapy, we at last have reason to be hopeful that serious criminality can be forestalled and perhaps, one day, even eradicated.

References

Bertin, C. (1982). *La Dernière Bonaparte*. Paris: Librairie Académique Perrin.

deMause, L. (1974). The evolution of childhood. In: Lloyd deMause (Ed.), *The History of Childhood* (pp. 1–73). New York: Psychohistory Press.

Kahr, B. (1994). The historical foundations of ritual abuse: an excavation of ancient infanticide. In: Valerie Sinason (Ed.), *Treating Survivors of Satanist Abuse* (pp. 45–56). London: Routledge.

Klein, M. (1932). *The Psycho-Analysis of Children*, trans. Alix Strachey. London: Hogarth Press and The Institute of Psycho-Analysis. [First published as *Die Psychoanalyse des Kindes*. Vienna: Internationaler Psychoanalytischer Verlag.]

Moellenhoff, F. (1966). Hanns Sachs, 1881–1947: the creative unconscious. In: F. Alexander, S. Eisenstein, & M. Grotjahn (Eds.), *Psychoanalytic Pioneers* (pp. 180–199). New York: Basic Books.

Nunberg, H., & Federn, E. (Eds.) (1962). *Minutes of the Vienna Psychoanalytic Society. Volume I: 1906–1908*, trans. Margarethe Nunberg. New York: International Universities Press.

Westwick, A. (1940). Criminology and Psychoanalysis. *Psychoanalytic Quarterly, 9*: 269–282.

EDITORS AND CONTRIBUTORS

Anne Aiyegbusi is a Consultant Nurse in the National Health Service who has worked as a senior nurse in a range of secure services. She has a particular interest in women's secure services and personality disorder, and is committed to applying some of the principles of therapeutic communities to secure forensic services. One focus of her interventions is to help clinicians, especially nurses, to work with the emotional impact associated with these services by providing space to think about the rich and complex phenomenology that is present within the forensic setting. She has published and made many conference presentations about the psychodynamics of forensic mental health nursing, and is currently undertaking PhD study of the nurse-patient relationship with people who have personality disorders.

David Armstrong is a Principal Consultant at the Tavistock Consultancy Service, the Tavistock and Portman NHS Foundation Trust. A collection of papers he has written over the past 15 years, *Organization in the Mind: Psychoanalysis, Group Relations and Organizational Consultancy*, edited by Robert French, was published by Karnac in 2005.

John Gordon is a Consultant Adult Psychotherapist in the National Health Service and works in a Forensic Psychotherapy Department; at the Cassel Hospital, a specialist personality disorder service; and in private practice. He is Lecturer in the Faculty of Continuing Education, Birkbeck College, University of London, and Honorary Senior Lecturer at Imperial College Medical School. He is a Member of the British Psychoanalytic Association, a Senior Member of the British Association of Psychotherapists, and a Member of the Institute of Group Analysis. He is co-author with Stuart Whiteley of *Group Approaches in Psychiatry* and is interested in the application of Bion's thinking on psychosis to clinical work in groups. His most recent contribution, "Some neglected clinical material from Bion's Experiences in Groups: a prototypal interpretation", will appear in *Bion Today*, edited by Chris Mawson.

Sharman Harding is a group analyst with an interest in the rehabilitation of offenders. She has worked as a group analyst in a secure forensic hospital and in a maximum security prison.

Professor R.D. Hinshelwood is a Member of the British Psychoanalytical Society, a Fellow of the Royal College of Psychiatrists, and currently Professor in the Centre for Psychoanalytic Studies, University of Essex, UK. Previously he was Clinical Director of the Cassel Hospital. He has written extensively on psychotherapeutic organisations, including *Suffering Insanity* (2004), which explores the impact of psychotic suffering on institutional dynamics, and *Locked in role* (1993), an analysis of institutional dynamics in a prison. He has been involved in therapeutic communities for many years, founding *The International Journal of Therapeutic Communities* in 1980; and he has also written on the work of Melanie Klein (*Dictionary of Kleinian Thought*, 1989; *Clinical Klein*, 1993). In 1984 he founded *The British Journal of Psychotherapy*, and in 1998 the journal *Psychoanalysis and History*.

Dr Gabriel Kirtchuk is a Consultant Psychiatrist in Psychotherapy (Forensic) and psychoanalyst. He has worked in forensic settings for the last fifteen years, and has established a Department of Forensic Psychotherapy within a medium-secure unit. The Department is based on psychodynamic and systemic principles, and has adopted an institutional, group, family and individual integrated approach. More recently, a semi-structured protocol of working in the transference/countertransference with multidisciplinary teams has been developed. For the last six years he has held the position of Lead Clinician of the National Forensic Psychotherapy Training and Development Strategy, and he is an Honorary Senior Lecturer at Imperial College Medical School.

Michael Mercer is a psychoanalyst and a Member of the British Psychoanalytical Society. He is on the staff of the Adult Department of the Tavistock and Portman NHS Trust, where he is Chair of the Department Clinical Services Committee. He trained as a social worker. He has experience of working in the Probation Service, and he has managed a Local Authority Mental Health Service. For a number of years he has worked as a consultant to an NHS Forensic Service.

Claire Miller qualified as a music therapist in 1997, having previously completed a music degree and a masters in the psychology of music. She has practised in areas of learning disability, neurodisability and, for over 9 years, forensic mental health services. She currently holds a Professional Development Lead post in a forensic mental health arts therapies service in the National Health Service.

Dr Carine Minne is a Consultant Psychiatrist in Forensic Psychotherapy at the Portman Clinic, Tavistock and Portman NHS Foundation Trust, and at Broadmoor Hospital, West London Mental Health NHS Trust. She is also a psychoanalyst and a member of the British Psychoanalytical Society.

Dr David Reiss is a Consultant Forensic Psychiatrist and Director of Forensic Psychiatry Education in a major NHS Forensic Mental Health Unit, as well as Honorary Clinical Senior Lecturer in the Division of Neuroscience and Mental Health at Imperial College London. He completed his higher training at the Maudsley Hospital, where he was subsequently appointed Consultant within the Traumatic Stress Service. He holds both an MPhil in Psychiatry and a Postgraduate Diploma in Forensic Psychiatry. He was formerly Director of the Forensic Psychiatry Teaching Unit at the Institute of

Psychiatry. He has published research papers on a variety of topics, including personality disorder, forensic psychiatry education, homicide inquiries and stalking.

Stanley Ruszczynski is a Consultant Adult Psychotherapist and Clinical Director of the Portman Clinic (Tavistock and Portman NHS Foundation Trust, London), an outpatient forensic psychotherapy clinic. He has acted as a clinical and organisational consultant in medium- and high-secure settings, in a prison and in other psychiatric settings, and is in private practice as a psychoanalytic psychotherapist. He is a Senior Member of the British Association of Psychotherapists and a Direct Member of the International Psychoanalytic Association. He has edited and co-edited five books, including *Intrusiveness and Intimacy in the Couple* with James Fisher (Karnac, 1995), *Psychoanalytic Psychotherapy in the Kleinian Tradition* with Sue Johnson (Karnac, 1999), and most recently *Lectures on Violence, Perversion and Delinquency* with David Morgan (Karnac, 2007). He is the author of over twenty-five book chapters and journal articles and is a past Joint Editor of the *Journal of the British Association of Psychotherapists*.

Gillian Tuck is a Practice Development Nurse in the National Health Service. She has worked in medium- and high-secure mental health services for the last seven years, specialising in the care of patients who have personality disorder. She has a particular interest in the psychodynamics of forensic mental health nursing, as well as in the use of a systems-psychodynamic approach to examining organisations. She has completed a masters degree in Consultation and the Organisation: Psychoanalytic Approaches at the Tavistock Clinic and University of East London.

Dr Kiriakos Xenitidis is a Consultant Psychiatrist at the South London and Maudsley NHS Trust. He works at the Mental Impairment Evaluation and Treatment Service (MIETS), a national secure inpatient unit based at the Bethlem Hospital for adults with neurodevelopmental disorders such as learning disabilities and autism. He also runs the adult Attention Deficit Hyperactivity Disorder Service, a national outpatient clinic at the Maudsley Hospital. He is a group analyst and is practising, writing and teaching on the applications of group analysis in adults with neurodevelopmental disorders. Dr Xenitidis is also an Honorary Senior Lecturer at the Section of Brain Maturation at the Institute of Psychiatry, London. His research interests include epidemiology, health services research and forensic aspects of developmental disorders.

FOREWORD

R.D. Hinshelwood

When I sat down to read this book, I decided to fasten my seat-belt. There are people so desperate that they are willing to commit terrible crimes to get their message across, and there are carers so assaulted that they must put safety before care. Not a book to read before bedtime, you might say. However, I'm not sure that this is setting the scene correctly, because when I read it, in addition to the psychopathology of desperation, there is the capacity to reflect on it, to give despair the meaning it should have, and to do so with a greatly reassuring power.

It would seem a truism to say that meeting someone with a major mental illness is disconcerting.[1] However familiar we are with this occurrence, we often forget that professional carers are just as vulnerable to such a difficult confrontation. It is as if we assumed that because they are professionals they will *only* have the proper caring feelings. We must not lose sight of the fact that certain jobs require work to be done on our own feelings, as well as doing work on the raw material. There is now an increasing sociological literature on "emotional labour", as it is called. In a service occupation, part of the job is to have the right feelings at the right times.[2]

This important issue of working with "raw material" that is other human beings is especially aggravated with those human beings who engage in disturbing relations to the point of such intolerability they have had to be incarcerated. The dilemma for prisons, mental hospitals, and their progeny, forensic psychiatric services, has always been how you carry on emotionally caring for the intolerable. The fact that it can be done is a tribute to the fortitude of the human spirit in general and of mental health workers in particular.

I have always been uncomfortable that such fortitude is not recognised as much as it should be. Hence I greatly welcome this volume, which directly acknowledges the human problems of dangerous caring, and investigates both its positive side (the view that countertransference can be positively useful) and the toll it imposes on the wellbeing of the carers. The book is a work in the "psychology of care". And it is a work that probes very deep into the complex interactions of the subjective experiences of the parties involved. These intersubjective encounters are examined at the interpersonal, group and organisational levels. Using the insights of object-relations psychoanalysis, great detail is found in the emotional labour required of carers in this work.

The BIG question hanging over all of the contributions is: How do people cope with this arduous labour? The answer all the way through is that we must make meaning of the experiences, both meaning in our own terms as carers and meaning in terms of those we care for. Perhaps it is the uniquely difficult aim of a psychoanalytic approach that these two brands of meaning should be compatible. What does it *mean* to say that a schizophrenic is like "a hunk of meat"? It is chilling to hear such a report, because it was, we imagine, chilling to have the experience. It is not unfamiliar; and in fact perhaps the commonest response is to recoil from the person as if they were no longer human. Having recoiled so, there are two avenues of advance on the problem. One is to proceed with some consistency by approaching that person as if he or she were not a person but an object in which certain disease processes or biochemical interactions are taking place—this is the approach of an objective science. The other approach, which might be characterised as a psychoanalytic one, is to relate this meaning—"this person is no longer a person"—to the meaning of the other person's experience as well, that is to say the patient also has a sense of not being a person.[3] This approach, being so attuned to the sensitive subjectivities of each partner, is often not endowed with the title of science. Whether or not it is comparable to objective science, it is very much more difficult, and the conditions for its successful outcome are in urgent need of attention. This book pays that attention.

We could say, as I think this book does, that the most useful vaccination against the impact of madness is to create meanings in its place. And the book goes further to say that the best of vaccines is the creation of shared meanings: meanings shared by the carer and the cared-for. As a result, the notion of reflective practice is at the centre of this book. Some units at least (Three Bridges, for instance) have instituted specific elements of the timetable which are designated "reflective groups" for staff. They are opportunities for the generation of meaning. Reflective practice (a common enough term in management practice) has special features in this manifestation. It concerns the reflection on experiences in the work which point towards *unconscious* processes. To my mind, the writers of these papers are absolutely correct that the reflection should be guided by the work; it is not an opportunity for the staff simply to free associate and abreact themselves. These reflective groups are places where the emotional labour of generating the meaning of one's personal reaction to the work is stimulated. Reflection must remain focused on some aspect of the work, and we are treated to many examples. However, it seems to me that we have to be realistic with regard to this ambition. Meanings are not always easy to come by. There is therefore a requirement that carers (like their patients) must live with some degree of meaninglessness, or with some substitute pseudo-meanings.

There is a further characteristic which underlies the whole of this book. That concerns the aim of creating *shared* meanings. It is common in contemporary psychoanalytic psychotherapy to assume that we are engaged in a process of "containment". If the process of containment is that the mind of the carer functions as an auxiliary organ of meaning generation, then its generation of meanings is a good and therapeutically beneficial service.

However, this is an assumption, and it may conceal the possibility that there are limits to containing. The work in these units could be used to investigate whether the assumption is true in all cases. In my view we need to address the question: In what sense is a new meaning for the suffering beneficial to a patient? Experience is accumulating that there may be two alternative answers to this. One answer was the original idea that new meaning is absorbed by the patient so that he acquires a new function within himself for making meanings out of his experiences. We now know that not all patients are as enthusiastic as others about absorbing a meaning-generating function. In other words, as John Steiner wrote, "I want to make a distinction between *understanding* and *being understood,* and point out that the patient who is not interested in acquiring understanding—that is, understanding about himself—may yet have a pressing need to be understood by the analyst" (1993, p. 132). This makes a lot of difference to the prognosis and the aims of treatment. A patient who may well appreciate that he is thought about and understood by his carers might simply leave it at that. Since he is not interested in understanding himself, the carer's understanding of him provides no long-term benefit, only a satisfaction for the moment. Carers need to know what their patient appreciates—either being thought about, or doing their own thinking. A patient only interested in being understood will always be coming back for more. In such cases, carers can become very frustrated when the patient simply remains dependent on the carers' emotional labouring, and doesn't "get better properly". So, in my view, the research reported in this book leads directly to further research on the early assessment of the patient's attitude to being understood (to depend on the auxiliary organ provided by the carer, or to introject the function as his own). There may have to be a further assessment about the logistics of resources to allow the long-term maintenance therapy of being understood—like insulin for the diabetic. In other words, should scarce resources be concentrated on those who might introject the function of self-understanding for themselves? I regard these questions as undecided, and think that such a body of researchers as those who have created this book should take their project this step further.

This dependence on "being understood" is really about the psychodynamics of chronicity, and in this connection I want to speculate about a further problem. Particularly for those patients incarcerated indefinitely in mental or other institutions, the very act of imprisonment has its own complex psychodynamics. There is not just the problem that custody and care can be conflicting elements—

a feature of these institutions remarked on consistently amongst these authors. There is another feature of residential care: the imprisonment renders the inmates totally dependent, helpless and vulnerable. The very basics of being fed, washed and exercised have to be supervised and controlled according to principles which are distant from the needs and the agency of the individual. This enforced helplessness is striking, but in my experience not as fully recognised as it might be. Many personalities, and particularly those who get themselves incarcerated in prisons or mental health services, are especially provoked by the forced infantilisation. Often coming from families and backgrounds where fending for themselves was a necessary accomplishment for survival, they have developed a defensive carapace, becoming hard, apparently invulnerable, and extremely resistant to recognising the vulnerable child side of their natures. Then forced dependency and helplessness is a particular assault on their desperate adjustment to life, and it leads to the customary reactions to the feeling of being assaulted: retaliatory assault, or an extremely passive kind of "playing dead". Neither of these reactions is particularly compatible with care as most carers conceive it; and most carers can themselves respond unhelpfully with frustration and forms of angry defensiveness or firm coercion. This reinforces the life experience of these patients which has made them suspicious of help and care, and they can exaggerate their compensatory pseudo-maturity. This cycle is a part of the catalogue of similar vicious circles that underlie chronicity.

Taking this a step further, the wisdom in this book is not confined to the simple notion of containment with which I was just occupied. If there are limits to the capacity to affect the minds of patients towards better *self*-understanding, there are other important levels of containment which several of the authors explore. If meaning-generation is a never-ending task with some (or many) patients, there is another aim. For staff too, meaninglessness is a serious burden; therefore, making their subjective interactions more coherent and understandable is an effective support against the stress of the work. Thus if there is an enduring need to drip-feed patients with understanding, staff can benefit from a continuous flow of understanding as well. They need a protection against the meaninglessness of the patient's experiences; they too need a psycho-insulin therapy!

Beyond this, there is an organisational level at which understanding has an important impact. It is clear that disturbed patients impact on staff to disturb them, and then in turn the disturbed staff members collectively influence the service, which becomes a disturbed service in its own right. This is now a well-known phenomenon. It was an unnerving experience to find my own papers on this topic referred to, often more succinctly and clearly than my original writing! If the collective disturbance of the service is prompted in part by how the staff become disturbed, then one contribution to sorting out the organisation is to contain the staff's disturbance better through understanding it. Thus reflective practice of this psychoanalytic kind can be a fitness schedule for the organisation itself. So the approach in this book has three levels at which it may operate: first on the mind of the receptive patient; then on the general morale of the staff; and finally on the organisational problems of the service itself.

As I have tried to make clear, it would be a mistake to pigeonhole these papers into the smallish world of forensic psychotherapy. It is a significant contribution to a much wider field. The subject of that field could be called the "psychology of care" in general, or at least the psychology of mental health care. There is a lot of that psychology about. We neglect it at our peril, and its general neglect makes the papers in this book all the more significant a contribution. But the book is important not just because it is a form of professional practice; it touches the human heart of one of the most emotionally arduous of all occupations.

Notes

1 For instance, I was struck by someone as sensitive as a Nobel Prize winner for literature who could respond to meeting a schizophrenic person by saying "He was a hunk of meat. There was no-one there" (quoted in Knowlson 1996, p. 209). Samuel Beckett used these words after a visit to Bethlem Royal Hospital in 1935, shortly after he had begun his own therapy at the Tavistock Clinic, with Wilfred Bion, in 1934.

2 Hochschild (1983) researched a form of training for this aspect of the job of airline cabin crew. Theodosius (2006) applied these ideas to nurses.

3 In Winnicott's terms, the schizophrenic person has suffered an interruption of his "continuity of being" (Winnicott 1960, p. 594).

INTRODUCTION

John Gordon and Gabriel Kirtchuk

Our main reason for writing this book is expressed starkly in an old country western song:

> You can't know the feelin'
> Inside me that is stealin'
> You can't know cause it don't show on me.
> You can't hear me sighin'
> Or see my heart a cryin'
> You can't know cause it don't show on me.
> Abused, unused, refused, misused
> That I got from you
> But you can't know the feelin'
> Cause it just don't show on me. [Buck Owens, 1956]

This contrast between powerful feelings inside and an almost total absence of outward expression—even a blanket taboo on such expression—characterizes the professional work ethic of many colleagues. To experience strong emotional reactions to patients, let alone to do so regularly or to discuss them in staff meetings, is equivalent to professional suicide.

If the above description of work in forensic settings sounds familiar, we think this book is for you. Even if you consider the formulation exaggerated, you may find the following chapters of interest. For, after all, contact with patients in a forensic context generates the most extreme emotional responses in staff, let alone the press or the public, of any in the always problematic interaction between mentally ill people and the community. The forensic patient's "index offence", that so technically antiseptic piece of institutional jargon which, like Pandora's box, conceals an inconceivable gamut of human suffering, violence and dread, once "out" has an almost unlimited capacity to contaminate anyone with ordinary human responsiveness. "Nameless dread" (Bion, 1962, p. 116) of such magnitude terrifies because it blows the mind.

Nevertheless, Bion suggested that it is vital, when two people get together for the purpose of trying to make sense of the life trajectory—including the calamities—of one of them, that both feel afraid: "In psychoanalysis, when approaching the unconscious—that is, what we do not know—we, patient and analyst alike, are certain to be disturbed. In every consulting room, there ought to be two rather frightened people: the patient and the psychoanalyst. If they are not both frightened, one wonders why they are bothering to find out what everyone knows" (Bion, 1976/2005. p. 104). Fear arises because they are seeking to discover something new and unknown, which could contribute a surprising and different way of understanding the patient's dilemmas. If the two people are comfortable, even complacent, there is obviously nothing new to find out—all is familiar, "obvious" and under control; nothing can happen.

A frequent echoing phrase in forensic ward rounds and nursing handovers is: "The patient is settled". Palpable relief precludes alarming untoward events, including new insights. But such relief is very understandable. For in the face of the "index offence" and the gnawing anxiety which it evokes in members of the multidisciplinary staff team, it is clear that once a patient has acted on a belief, impulse or delusion so as to damage another person catastrophically, there can never be an absolute reassurance which rules out a repetition. Consequently, fear may become not an inevitable accompaniment of an open state of mind but a permanent and incapacitating terror. Of course this is only if emotional responses are "allowed" by the members of the multidisciplinary team. But who would find it possible to be aware of such intense anxieties or of revulsion, hatred and disgust, let alone of other disturbing—but also very understandable—responses: excitement, sexual interest, fascination, love? And how might multidisciplinary staff teams operate on the basis that, not only could individual members sustain their emotional experiences, but the team as a group could sustain its members in doing so; further, that the organization as a whole could acknowledge and sanction this emotional work as an essential part of the professional task?

Our premise is that there is a way for multidisciplinary staff teams to face the emotional strains of work with forensic patients. For many years we, and the colleagues who have joined us to write this book, have worked closely with patients and staff in a wide range of forensic settings within the National Health Service. Through our particular experience on secure wards, we have developed a deep appreciation of the difficulties of maintaining emotional contact with forensic patients—for all staff, but especially for nurses whose role requires them to bear the brunt of such contact over long periods of time.

The authors' training and general clinical experience has familiarized them with the countertransference: the unconscious effects on the worker's feelings, thoughts and behaviour of the patient's symptoms, actions, history, communications and impacts. The title of the book includes the words "psychic assaults" to convey the often shocking collision which underlies a simple meeting between two people, a patient and a staff member. To remain unaware, to render oneself oblivious, or to hide one's reactions from others, however understandable, deprives the worker of valuable information—not only about oneself but about the patient. We realized that if we could make the concept of countertransference accessible to our multidisciplinary staff colleagues, we might offer a dimension for understanding the patient that would contribute to their task: "handover" could become a more comprehensive and useful account of the patient's state of mind and risk.

In clinical work with forensic patients who are frequently themselves out of touch with what has happened in their lives (both to themselves and to others), the worker's awareness of his or her feelings is often the main vehicle for understanding the patients' emotional states, psychopathology and offending behaviours.

Particularly in people with psychotic illnesses or when the offence has been compartmentalized and split-off ("lacks insight"), the emotional meanings often only become available in the fine grain of interactions on the ward, in casual encounters with patients, in the kitchen or during medication rounds. And staff members' emotional responses—*if they can be permitted and subjected to careful exploration and sustained reflection by the staff team*—can be significant clues to these meanings. Most importantly, risk assessment and management, those intrinsic and constant elements of the task in forensic settings, can be vitally informed by such countertransference-based understandings.

A more extensive discussion of aspects of the development of the concept of countertransference in psychoanalytic thinking can be found in the following chapters. Here we would highlight that in Freud's earliest references to the countertransference (1910, 1912), emphasis was placed on how the unconscious impingement of unresolved personal emotional conflicts and issues interfered with and severely jeopardized the professional attitude towards psychoanalytic work with patients. Just as we have indicated above, the clinician considered his or her subjective reactions to be at best irrelevant to the work in hand, or more ominously to indicate serious, shameful and probably culpable obstacles to ethical practice. Certainly, strong feelings in the worker interfered with a poised concern essential for carrying out his or her roles and tasks as set out in professional and government codes and guidelines. The possibility that clinicians' feelings and responses, however superficial or dysfunctional, could also represent the tip of an iceberg of meanings underlying a patient's internal conflicts and maladaptive relationship patterns was not salient as long as countertransference was fundamentally considered to be unconscious bias or blind spot: a distorting lens on reality, like the patient's transference.

From around 1950, however, psychoanalytic theoretical understanding—and even more importantly, the evolution of clinical practice—began to focus intensively on how even the worker's most idiosyncratic, bizarre or deeply disorientating emotional states and thoughts could be examined for clues to the patient's (usually unvoiced) experiences and predicaments. It is precisely this aspect of the countertransference, gradually revealing a potential block, distortion or impasse which threatens the professional task as the very means to move forward, that we intend to illustrate in this book. We also show how we have elaborated a multifaceted intervention strategy, which can inform the orientation of Departments of Forensic Psychotherapy, to integrate a capacity to work with the countertransference at individual, group, ward milieu, multidisciplinary team and forensic service (organizational) levels. But for the moment enough of theory! Here are two everyday examples of work in forensic settings to give you the flavour of what you will find in the rest of the book.

The kidnapped occupational therapist

A young female occupational therapist of Mexican origin presents to her reflective practice group (a weekly meeting of nurses or multidisciplinary staff where they discuss their work with a member of the Forensic Psychotherapy Department). She has been working with a male patient from a conflict-ridden, murderously authoritarian state who had been persecuted in his country, escaped by means of a forged passport and arrived here. He embarked on a relationship with a South American woman which she eventually brought to an end. The patient responded by abducting her and her new boyfriend, who were held hostage until they freed themselves and escaped. The patient was convicted and sent to prison, where he developed paranoid delusions and had to be transferred to a secure ward. He complied well, after some time seemed to be symptom-free, and at an upcoming tribunal it was assumed by the patient and the staff team that he would be released.

While awaiting this anticipated outcome, the patient singled out the occupational therapist, whom he asked to help with food shopping and kitchen skills as part of a self-catering assessment. The occupational therapist was pleased to help her patient, but she began to feel exceedingly uncomfortable when he offered insistently to prepare food for her. Before a meeting with her, the patient was heard by a student on placement on the ward to say that he "was going for something good now".

Preoccupied with her unabated discomfort, the occupational therapist wondered whether she should end her relationship with the patient. Her unease reflected both her awareness that somehow the boundaries of their relationship had shifted and her conviction that stopping at that point would let the patient down. She was struggling with strong feelings of guilt for not being "professional enough" to manage the work; but she also sensed, after some experience in the reflective group where staff members' personal reactions were highly valued, that something was coming from the patient to stir up these particular thoughts and feelings: her own capacity and propensity to have just these specific feelings and responses were being recruited by the patient's contribution to their encounters.

Our view is that this occupational therapist's sensitive resonance to her patient's impacts amounts to the hidden insight that, despite his manifest improvement in the opinion of all concerned, he continues to be engaged subtly in the re-enactment of his crime. He is hijacking a "couple" (originally the ex-girlfriend and her new boyfriend) in two ways. First, through the process of singling out and "specialing" his occupational therapist, the patient separates her from the team, for she is still tempted to hide her most distressing "unprofessional" inclinations, if not from herself then at least from her colleagues until supported by considerable experience in the reflective practice group. If this opportunity for collaborative reflection had not been possible, she would have remained unintegrated with her team. Second, a potentially creative relationship between a "couple", the patient and the occupational therapist in her role of helping the patient to improve his kitchen skills, is "kidnapped" when the patient subtly but insistently changes the boundaries of their task so as to convert it into an intimate dinner together. The kidnapping is repeated over and over again, out of sight but not out of the insight of the occupational therapist into her subjective states combined with her "coupling"/linking with the reflective practice group in order to give them explicit meanings.

Significantly, at first the team considered this occupational therapist's reactions to be an entirely personal "hiccup" and advised her to withdraw from the patient. Changing the primary nurse of a patient and transferring staff to another ward are very frequent consequences of the kind of emotional entanglement just described. And with the departing staff member go vital clues: not only is the possibility lost for a more comprehensive understanding of the patient by the multidisciplinary team, but crucial information which could inform risk assessment remains uninterpreted. Why, for example, was this particular occupational therapist picked? The patient considered his South American ex-girlfriend as submissive. Therefore it is likely that not only was the occupational therapist's national origin relevant in her selection, but the respective position of her professional group within the multidisciplinary team—peripheral if not subordinate—conditioned the patient's preference and added to the probability that the meanings enacted by his choice would pass unnoticed: he might now get away with abduction.

"Shut up, it's too much"

A male nurse spoke in his reflective practice group about finding the staff toilet on the rehabilitation ward smeared with shit. He worried about the effects on his female colleagues; but when he began to elaborate a disturbing fantasy about a specific male patient and the nurse's own wife, his nursing colleagues became extremely uneasy. They told him to stop, it was too much and he should just shut up. Later in supervision, the group analyst who had been facilitating the group described his sense of paralysis. He realized that something emotionally significant about the patient and his impulses could be emerging through the nurse's reactions to the recounted episode on the ward, but he felt too uncomfortable to intervene. When subsequently the patient was moved to an acute ward, where he behaved impeccably, conflict broke out between the staff teams regarding the appropriateness of the transfer. Thus emotional disturbance in the mind of a nursing staff member rippled through his nursing group, only to be reiterated between the two wards at the organizational level of the forensic service.

We believe it is very significant that a "couple" also appears, and very explicitly, in our second example. We did not choose intentionally to call attention to this feature; rather, a common theme emerged out of our awareness in the selection and writing of this chapter. And we do want to emphasize that, on reflection, the role of the couple, more abstractly formulated as a link, is of paramount importance in forensic work. Many, perhaps most patients encountered on forensic wards have psychotic features (schizophrenia and paranoid states are most frequent) exclusively or in combination with personality disorders, including perversions and antisocial tendencies. In all of these conditions, the link (attachment) between the patient and other people; between the patient and his own thoughts, feelings, experiences and history; between the patient as an individual and the social groups—including the ward milieu—to which he belongs: these links are all seriously disturbed, distorted, attacked or obliterated.

This is why we focus in this book on the countertransference, the countertransference conceived as a link between the patient and the responsive mind and sensibilities of the staff. Whatever the patient does, the staff member—if attuned to his or her responses—resurrects inchoate or virtually "murdered" and "perverted" remnants of human responsiveness, whether the patient wishes this or not. The patient cannot help but affect the staff member; this is entirely up to the latter, who consequently acquires a means within his or her own mind of sustaining a link of ongoing concerned inquiry into the patient's personality even when the patient takes external flight.

Of course the other side of this coin is that no professional is basically immune from emotional contagion. Immunity is only achieved secondarily, as an attempt to protect and anaesthetize oneself. The group analyst in our second example, who knew theoretically about the countertransference, as well as the psychoanalysts and nurses who have written the chapters which make up this book—all of them struggle constantly with their emotional reactions and their inevitable reflex to evade them. We are all frightened clinicians; and—especially in forensic settings—we all need containing (Bion, 1970), reflective spaces (Hinshelwood, 1994) so that we can attend to our countertransferences, give them meaning, and thereby more fully invigorate our professional roles.

So our two vignettes mark out the ground—individual emotional reactions (links) to patients, their combined effects on small groups of staff, and their escalating and maladaptive resonance within the wider forensic organization—which we intend to cover in this book. We will try to clarify the concept of countertransference through many more clinical examples, and from their varied perspectives the authors of each chapter will show how they use the countertransference to understand patients, to work with staff groups and to consult to forensic institutions. Anne Aiyegbusi and Gillian Tuck describe vicious cycles of extreme emotional impact between patients and nurses: the trauma of everyday life on the ward. Carine Minne focuses on her psychoanalytically informed work with an exceptionally disturbed patient to show how the analyst struggles to find, and mind, her patient through attending to the countertransference. John Gordon discusses group psychotherapy on secure wards, based on material presented in supervision by Sharman Harding, Claire Miller and Kiriakos Xenitidis, which illustrates the overwhelming effect of countertransference on clinical work and on the supervisory process. Michael Mercer describes his reflective practice groups for staff in management roles and explores how the countertransference can interfere with managers' capacity to perceive crucial organizational dynamics, clarify tasks for subordinates and take appropriate decisions. Stan Ruszczynski reviews the psychoanalytic theory of containment in the light of the specific emotional burdens evoked in staff by patients with personality disorders and sexual perversions, and he argues that consultation to the forensic institution as a whole is required to sustain its primary function as a container of toxic dread. Gabriel Kirtchuk, David Reiss and John Gordon consider the inevitable institutional and professional fragmentation in forensic settings. They present their development of a common language, focused on interpersonal dynamics, which can help to integrate multidisciplinary teams as they work to assess and monitor risk, devise coherent treatment interventions and establish emotional contact with patients. Finally, John Gordon and Gabriel Kirtchuk consider the role of a Forensic Psychotherapy Department (and, by implication, of a Consultant Forensic Psychotherapist) within the forensic institution. They highlight the countertransference as a central orienting principle and summarize the clinical and training interventions which can support forensic staff and services to contain and learn from their emotional experiences with patients.

CHAPTER ONE

Caring amid victims and perpetrators: trauma and forensic mental health nursing

Anne Aiyegbusi and Gillian Tuck

Introduction

Patients detained in secure mental health services are often a severely traumatised population. A typical picture is of childhood histories characterised by severe abuse, neglect and loss preceding adult lives equally full of destructiveness such as family violence, self-injury, substance abuse and criminality. Although requiring secure care, these patients are often difficult to care for because they frequently interpret acts of care in distorted ways. Their behavioural disturbance may be extreme, but it is the way they communicate by impact that nursing staff find so difficult to work with. Because of the patients' highly disturbed early parenting, the risk of traumatic re-enactment within care-giving relationships is high. Perhaps for that reason, allegations of cruelty, neglect and sexual abuse on the part of nursing staff are routine in the life of such services.

Consequently, employment within secure mental health services may present a risk to the mental health of nursing staff, especially those who may be drawn unconsciously to work with this population because of their own unresolved trauma histories. Nurses are not routinely trained to understand or work effectively with severe psychological trauma, and the patients' presentations may not have been conceptualised from the perspective of trauma. Yet nursing staff, in an interpersonal sense, are at the front line of services for groups of people who have been massively traumatised in some of the most horrific ways imaginable. Furthermore, the work of nursing staff takes place within the patients' social environments, where contact with difficult-to-process emotional material occurs unpredictably. At the very worst, the social environments of hospital wards and other hospital areas come to replicate the patients' internal worlds.

This chapter will describe in more detail some of the psychodynamics that are commonplace in secure services. Specifically, we discuss the ways in which patients' traumatic histories impact on nursing practice and nursing staff, and show how a model of psychological containment can assist nurses in their primary task. All case examples are fictional but nevertheless represent accurately the clinical phenomena of trauma as experienced by forensic patients and nurses who come into close contact within secure institutions.

Trauma

Trauma can be defined as a wound or piercing of the skin. The term was used as a metaphor by Freud (1920) to describe how the psyche can be pierced when overwhelming affective stimuli, such as extreme fear resulting from a life-threatening environmental event, break through the protective shield and overwhelm the ego's capacity to process the experience effectively. Conditions that would bring about such a traumatic situation may involve, for example, an individual being forced into the position of victim of violence by another. We think that the impact of traumatic experience is of special importance to forensic nurses whose clinical work includes the use of self (their personal responses, feelings and sensibilities) as a therapeutic tool for delivering mental health care to populations who have usually been both victims and perpetrators of trauma.

As Garland points out, "it is clear that the history of psychoanalysis and the development of Freud's understanding of trauma are linked" (1998, p. 13). Freud made a critical and arguably seminal contribution to the theoretical evolution of psychological trauma as a concept for understanding the clinical presentation of some psychiatric patients (1920). He hypothesized that a common developmental antecedent was shared by his adult patients who presented with hysteria: the experience of childhood sexual abuse. Freud also identified an important factor in the process of traumatisation, which was that symptoms tended to occur long after the traumatic event had taken place (*ibid.*). Therefore, an event occurring in early childhood may not immediately lead to symptoms. Symptoms may only appear at adolescence or during adult life. Freud postulated that the process which leads from traumatic experience to hysterical symptomatology involves primarily an unconscious memory of the event (*ibid.*). Memory of painful experience cannot be processed by the ego and so is repressed. Feelings originally experienced at the time of the traumatic event are cut off from consciousness or "strangulated", but they remain active in the unconscious and emerge as physical symptoms for which there is no organic cause.

By 1926, Freud had elaborated his theory of anxiety, which was previously understood as stemming from undischarged libidinal excitement. Freud now relocated anxiety within the ego, which formed part of his new paradigm of the mind consisting of id, ego and superego. According to Freud's model, the ego can differentiate between two important but separate types of anxiety. The first type is automatic anxiety and is experienced in actual situations of danger. The second type is signal anxiety and is experienced when there is a threat of danger. When external traumatic events occur, anxiety overwhelms the mind's defences against it. However, the source of overwhelming anxiety is also internal. Freud identified five primary internal anxieties common to everyone: birth, castration, loss of the loved object, loss of the object's love and annihilation anxiety. It is the interaction of the anxiety provoked by external events and the primary internal anxieties that are overwhelming to the mind and can be damaging to the personality.

The protective shield

Freud (1920) described the importance of a theoretical construct, the "protective shield", which he viewed as enveloping the mind to modulate both internal and external stimuli in order to maintain a manageable equilibrium of mental activity. The protective shield is initially provided through effective maternal care during earliest life.

Khan (1963) describes the concept of cumulative trauma as the result of many minor breaches in the role of the mother as protective shield throughout the child's development from infancy until adolescence. According to Khan, "cumulative trauma thus derives from the strains and stresses that an infant-child experiences in the context of his ego-dependence on the mother as his protective shield and auxiliary ego" (1963, p. 46). The "protective shield" function includes both the mother's personal involvement in modulating the degree of stimulus the infant receives and her management of the external environment. Breaches of the protective shield at this stage are not individually traumatic; rather, they can be thought of as somewhat minor stresses and strains. These minor breaches do not have the effect of damaging the ego, though they may bias it (Khan, 1963).

Through good enough maternal care, an individual eventually identifies with and internalises the protective shield and is able to modulate her own internal and external stimuli in a way which ensures that she keeps safe from harmful events which risk overwhelming feelings of fear, anxiety or anger. As Freud originally explained, traumatic events overwhelm the protective shield. However, Garland (1998) suggests this may not be sufficient to explain the full complexity of trauma. It is the collapse of a belief about the predictability of the world and the ability or preparedness of good objects to provide protection from harm that underpins the long-term, negative consequences on the personality that characterises the severely traumatised.

Individual vulnerability and re-enactment

As Garland has stated (1998), the impact of the traumatic event on an individual cannot be explained by the nature of the event alone. The interaction between the event and its subjective meanings within the individual's internal world is crucial. Furthermore, the occurrence of a traumatic event at a particular stage of development may leave an individual vulnerable to certain interpersonal relationships and life events which unconsciously resemble earlier patterns. For example, Garland refers to "activities that involve a disavowed risk" (1998, p. 23), when carelessness with the self may repeat an identification with a neglectful object. In this way, the unconscious function of repeating and re-enacting (directly or with reversed roles) the traumatic experience may be to avoid or conquer unbearable and unprocessed feelings such as powerlessness (Garland, 1998). For forensic patients, either bringing about a traumatic event or repeating their own trauma may be evident in the index offence.

Case example 1

Candice, who is currently detained in a high-security psychiatric hospital, was a victim of childhood sexual abuse by her violent, alcoholic father in a family where her victimisation was known about but no one intervened on her behalf. Her mother in particular turned a blind eye to her pain, while also failing in her role as protector for Candice. By the time Candice was fifteen years old, she was habitually placing herself in positions of vulnerability to being victimised. She would go for nights out alone in seedy drinking establishments where she would allow herself to be picked up by men. She was particularly prone to having brief sexual encounters with considerably older men. On one occasion when she was drunk and walking home alone late at night, she was assaulted by a stranger who forced her to perform an act of oral sex on him.

It could be argued that Candice had internalised a neglectful primary carer and so failed to keep herself safe in fundamental ways, just as her mother had failed to keep her safe in a most basic sense. However, Candice was also replicating her traumatic relationship with a violent, alcoholic, sexually abusing father in her own drunken, casual sexual activity with older men. All of these factors were present in the sexual assault. In addition, there was evidence of her own self-destructiveness and a re-enactment of previous trauma, all of which are phenomena to be found in the complex functioning of some traumatised people. Garland (1998) explains that whether unconsciously sought out or not, there is no difference in the quality of pain felt by the victim, who is no less traumatised for the fact that she may unconsciously have brought about her own trauma.

Candice was admitted to a medium-secure unit at the age of 17, following an offence of attempted murder where she throttled her lover during sexual intercourse. The offence could be understood as a re-enactment of the violence done to her when she was sexually assaulted. This time Candice was perpetrator rather than victim. She had therefore converted passive into active as a defence against unbearable feelings of powerlessness, which is another aspect of this tragedy that is common to the repetition of trauma. Reversal may be an attempt to relocate the horrendous psychic pain of victimisation into another who is felt to be able to take it. Additionally, reversal may involve revenge, and it may be the only way a traumatised person has of communicating how they feel, given the wordless nature of trauma (Garland 1998).

Case example 2

James is currently serving a prison sentence for child abduction and assault. As a child, he was the victim of sexual abuse by his foster father. He is now able to speak of his feelings of abject terror when his foster father held a knife to his throat when he attempted to resist the sexual advances. However, the offence that led to his incarceration in prison involved him abducting a child at knifepoint. He told his therapist that in one moment, when he looked the child in the eye while holding a knife up to his throat, he knew that "a connection had been made" and that his victim knew exactly how James felt. James had been trying for many years to understand feelings he had been struggling with, and he had tried many times to explain to other people what it felt like to be him. At the time of his offence James was not able to link his longstanding attraction to knives and his desire to harm others with knives to his own childhood experience of terror. The first time he was able to communicate this was when he instilled terror into someone else, another vulnerable child.

The form of communication employed by James is called projective identification (Klein, 1946) and is a very primitive method —often the only possible one—of expressing unmanageable feelings by locating them in others rather than in oneself. Alternatively, James' use of a vulnerable child to re-enact his own past traumatic experiences could be considered as an example of identification with the aggressor (Anna Freud, 1946). Identification with the aggressor can also involve directing traumatic acts towards the self in masochistic behaviour.

In addition to fantasising about threatening and stabbing other people with knives and his index offence, which involved abducting and making actual threats to another in such a horrific way, James also harms himself by making lacerations to his throat. Prior to imprisonment, he would use kitchen knives. In prison he has not had access to knives but uses any other sharp objects he can get hold of to inflict harm upon himself, including fingernails. He feels immensely powerful and in control when he hurts himself, in clear identification with his aggressor.

James has spent much of his sentence in the health care centre. In the earlier part of his sentence, prior to seeing his therapist, James regularly acted out. In particular, he would inflict wounds upon himself while subjecting prison nursing staff to shocking experiences. For example, once he could not be woken up by nurses, who feared he might be physically ill. A member of nursing staff pulled back James' bed covers to find that James had cut his throat. Reeling with shock, the nurse felt traumatised by this experience and required counselling and time away from the health care centre in order to recover.

Trauma and development

Sugarman (1994) describes how there is an interrelationship between trauma and development and that, as a general rule, the earlier the traumatic event occurs, the more debilitating the impact is likely to be. For example, conditions that cause disruption to the relationship between mother and child during the first eighteen months of a child's life may impact negatively on interpersonal relationships, self-esteem, sense of reality and personal identity. The stage of a person's development at the time of traumatic events may also determine whether an event is indeed traumatic or not. Additionally, a person's developmental stage may determine the form trauma symptoms will take.

Case example

Bradford's mother committed suicide in his presence when Bradford was one year old. The suicide was experienced as a violent attack on the infant. Because of his stage of development, Bradford internalised this violent attack by his primary carer (identified himself with his mother's actions) and as a result re-enacted this violence in all of his most intimate relationships. He severely beat three of his girlfriends, eventually leading to convictions for violence. Bradford was convicted of killing his eldest daughter while in a psychotic state. He was admitted to a medium-secure unit where the primary concern was his psychotic illness, which was treated with medication.

However, when Bradford's mental state stabilised, pronounced interpersonal difficulties became apparent to his clinical team. He became angry when his female primary nurse was not available to him. When his primary nurse was on leave, Bradford would make complaints about her and criticise her nursing skills, suggesting that he would have been discharged earlier were it not for his useless primary nurse. When his primary nurse was on duty, Bradford seemed to spend a lot of his time trying to distract her from other tasks in order that she spend more of her time talking to him about his problems and needs. Bradford's primary nurse was at a loss as to how to help him, and often felt pressurised as a result of his persistent attempts to secure her undivided attention.

In an attempt to manage Bradford's overdependence, the primary nurse, in conjunction with the ward psychologist, developed a programme whereby Bradford could have a fifteen-minute one to one session with his primary nurse each day that she was on duty, when he could raise anything that was on his mind. Unfortunately, Bradford's primary nurse was not able to stick to the planned fifteen minutes one day because of a disturbance on the ward. When she emerged from the incident, she was assaulted by Bradford, who later said that he was enraged because his expectations had been raised and then he had been "dumped".

Trauma and forensic populations

The preceding examples show that trauma occupies a central place in understanding the psychopathology of forensic patients. Clearly, in addition to being victims of traumatic events, they have also perpetrated them: traumatic pathology is intrinsically interpersonal in nature. That is, these patients have received failed early care and have been traumatised at the hands of early carers. The perpetration of traumatic offending on victims who are either actual intimates or who represent intimates who have been severely rejecting or abusive in the past thus represents the most vicious of vicious cycles in forensic settings (Adshead, 2004).

Case example

Zena was physically abused and abandoned by her mother before she was a year old. Zena is full of rage but cannot verbalise or explain her feelings. Her index offence involved setting fire to the home of a former probation officer. She was said to have been devastated when this probation officer, with whom she felt secure, changed jobs and relinquished her professional involvement with Zena. We believe Zena's act was a powerful communication of the non-verbal rage associated with her early abuse and abandonment by her mother. It was "ignited" when she felt abandoned by her probation officer.

Zena has been a patient in the high-security psychiatric hospital for five years. During that time she has changed wards fifteen times. A typical pattern is that a new nurse begins to work enthusiastically with Zena, who initially refuses to be involved. The nurse then puts in extra effort to establish a relationship, and Zena starts to respond positively. The nurse then begins to feel emotionally drained when Zena escalates her demands and acting out, which seem designed to retain the nurse as her personal carer at all times. When the nurse begins to resist, Zena makes threats of harm, and the care team decide to transfer her to a different ward to ensure the safety of the nurse. On the new ward, the process begins again.

Zena repeatedly experiences abandonment from her primary carer as soon as she reveals her neediness, and the organisation unwittingly facilitates the re-enactment by transferring Zena. However, it could be argued that by failing to recognise and respond to Zena's plight in a more appropriate way, the organisation also repeatedly exposes nurses to the emotionally gruelling task of trying to care for her without adequate skills or resources. This is also a negative emotional experience.

Adshead (1998) explains how the "maladaptive" behaviours of some disturbed psychiatric patients can be understood in terms of traumatic re-enactments of earlier rejection and abuse by primary caregivers. According to Adshead (*ibid.*), such behaviour may also reflect their unconscious attempt to gain mastery over overwhelming affect. This clearly seems to be the case with Zena, who attempts to manage fear of rejection while in a position of dependency on a caregiver by at first controlling the caregiver's movements. Adshead describes how projective identification "is most likely to be used by those individuals who lacked an attachment figure who could contain and soothe their arousal" (*ibid.*, p. 67). Zena had experienced massive pain and abandonment by a fear-inducing and non-containing primary object. In addition to contributing to the re-enactment of her abandonment within the institution, she also communicates her pain, rage and helplessness to her current carer. This usually happens as soon as she senses withdrawal on the part of the primary nurse. Withdrawal may occur either because the primary nurse is planning to take leave or because she is recoiling from Zena's overwhelming need to control the object. The primary nurse may not even be aware of her withdrawal, but Zena is aware because of an increased sensitivity to such interpersonal relationships which she has experienced many times before.

Trauma, forensic patients and forensic mental health services

Davies makes the following critical observation about the functioning of teams in forensic services:

> The view is taken that professionals who deal with offenders are not free agents but potential actors who have been assigned roles in the individual offender's own re-enactment of their internal world drama. The professionals have the choice not to perform, but they can only make this choice when they have a good idea what the role is they are trying to avoid. Until they can work this out, they are likely to be drawn into the play, unwittingly and therefore not unwillingly. Because of the latter, if the pressure to play is not anticipated, then the professional will believe he is in a role of his choosing. [1996, p. 133]

Davies' observation appears to be particularly salient in the case of traumatised forensic patients. The experience of nurses working in forensic mental health services is that the organisation (and therefore professionals at all levels) becomes embroiled in the internal world drama of highly traumatised patients. Perhaps this is all the more intense when a large number of highly traumatised people are interacting together, and hypothetically they may be creating together a particularly powerful traumatic scenario. Because of the power of re-enactment, and where there is an absence of theoretical frameworks to take account of this phenomenon, the repetition of trauma is inevitable.

Case example 1

Jacqueline was admitted to the high-security psychiatric hospital following an index offence of robbery at knifepoint. She had jumped out from an alleyway in broad daylight and held a knife to the throat of a female shopper whom she had approached from behind. Jacqueline robbed her victim, forcing her to hand over her purse and all other valuables. Throughout her childhood, Jacqueline had been the victim of particularly sadistic sexual abuse by her stepfather and by a residential social carer when she had been removed from her family. When Jacqueline committed her index offence, she was sixteen years old and had just been discharged from the children's home where the latter abuse had taken place. Jacqueline was symbolically re-enacting her trauma as perpetrator. Soon after being detained in the high-security psychiatric hospital, she formed a close relationship with a male offender who had committed many offences against young women. Although aware of the potential dangers, the institution did not discourage this relationship.

When Jacqueline was thirty-seven years old she was still detained in hospital but had undertaken weekly psychotherapy for more than a decade. It was at this time that Jacqueline disclosed to her carers that, while in hospital, she and her boyfriend had been engaging in extreme sado-masochistic activity of a type that directly replicated the abuse she suffered at the hands of her stepfather and the residential care worker. This activity had taken place within ward environments and at social events. Additionally, in talking about her childhood abuse within her family of origin, Jacqueline disclosed that her mother and grandmother had often been present but had failed to intervene on her behalf. It may be argued that professionals within the institution had unwittingly become drawn into Jacqueline's internal world and replicated the dynamics of her family by failing to ensure Jacqueline's safety from a violent male offender. Thus they unconsciously adopted the role of the non-protective maternal figure who turned a blind eye and allowed her to be intimate with such a dangerous man. This case example highlights the reasons why professionals working with people who have been victims and perpetrators of severe trauma require both a theoretical framework that takes account of the dynamics of psychological trauma and regular opportunities to meet together to reflect on their interactions.

As Garland (1998) makes clear, the treatment of traumatised people requires the therapist to function as container. When a person's internal world is in a state of disarray, she requires an external container which, over a period of time, she is able to internalise in order to regain a sense of internal regulation and stability. Importantly, a container enables a person to think about, rather than continually act out, their trauma. This task can be difficult to achieve, especially in the face of the fears, mistrust and rage that the traumatised person may need to experience in relation to the therapist. In the case of hospitalised forensic patients with whom we are accustomed to working, the same can be said for the nursing staff working in their social environment. Where there are groups of massively traumatised forensic patients residing together, the task of providing containment within interpersonal relationships can be all the more challenging. Garland (*ibid.*) explains that the task of containment involves neither recoiling from what the patient says nor becoming overwhelmed by the material. The implication is that the emotional impact of bearing witness to the narrative of trauma that a patient may recall, as well as to the affect that may accompany it, may be too difficult for the professional to bear without reacting with either rejection or collusion. This dynamic is standard among nursing staff working within forensic mental health services, and may indeed form the basis of conflict between professional carers.

Case example 2

Georgina grew up in a home where her alcoholic parents frequently engaged in violence between themselves. In this domestic setting Georgina was also regularly beaten up. She was admitted to the high-security psychiatric hospital following repeated acts of physical violence towards nurses in other mental health settings. This was repeated in the high-security psychiatric hospital, where a pattern was observed. Georgina would target nurses whom she thought were dismissive of her and her distress. On the other hand, she would be ingratiating to other nurses, who often received small gifts from her as tokens of her gratitude. This second group was extremely sympathetic towards Georgina and could often be observed cuddling her or holding her hand. Nurses who were victimised by Georgina were felt by their more favoured colleagues to be deserving of the treatment she meted out to them. The more favoured colleagues were in turn thought of as being manipulated by Georgina and as being unprofessional in the way they failed to maintain their boundaries. The fact was that the two groups, now in bitter conflict, had been drawn into replicating the acrimonious family environment in which Georgina grew up and was so traumatised. Collusion had replaced containment, and Georgina's acting out was consequently not in the least diminished.

Organisations and trauma

Organisations tasked with the care of highly traumatised and traumatising forensic patients are required to manage the internal and external demands made on them in a thoughtful and sensitive way. For instance, providing care and treatment for high-profile offenders means balancing the demands for public protection with the needs of the individual patients. Whilst the admission of patients to high-security institutions may serve to protect the public and create safer communities, the patients' traumatic experiences are still very much present and continue to exist in the organisation in an overwhelming and unprocessed form.

As the clinical examples highlight, it is often impossible for traumatised individuals to put their distress and pain into words. Instead they depend on our most primitive, yet extremely effective means of unconscious communication known as projective identification (Klein, 1946). This communication by impact—a term coined by Casement (1985)—may take many forms, including the repetition and reversal of trauma (Garland, 1998). As such, the nursing group tasked with the treatment of traumatised patients is required to withstand painful countertransference experiences. To process such intolerable suffering is challenging and difficult work, requiring a great deal of clinical experience, theoretical knowledge and support (Garland, *ibid.*). Yet many nurses, particularly those on the front line, are required to undertake this task for prolonged periods of time without, for example, the structure and the boundaries that may be provided by the therapeutic hour. In addition, front line nursing staff are the least likely to be specifically trained to manage this task or to have access to adequate supervision and support (Cox, 1996).

With this in mind, it is unsurprising that many staff are profoundly affected by their work. On the receiving end of patients' powerful projections, they also become distressed and defend themselves through the use of projection (Obholzer & Roberts, 1994). A paranoid-schizoid projective system is established (Halton, 1994) in which it is impossible to think about things in a more real and integrated way. Consequently, the whole organisation becomes caught up in the same distressed state of mind as the patients, overwhelmed by the trauma and unable to think.

The immense emotional pressures expelled during the process of projective identification often result in the recipient acting out her countertransferential feelings. Accordingly, the professional task can be neglected, or at worst perverted, such as in the re-enactment of patients' past traumatic experiences (Adshead, 1998). These re-enactments may manifest at an individual, group or organisational level. Examples include boundary violations, physical or sexual abuse, rejection and disempowerment. Yet the patient's projections are only part of the picture when thinking about complex organisational dynamics relating to trauma. Staff members will also have personal experiences of trauma and seek to repair the damage through processes of repetition and reversal. It can become particularly problematic when staff members' own traumas interact with those of patients, which in extreme cases can lead to psychological breakdown in both patients and staff.

These extreme incidents require much thought, but there is also a more subtle, yet pervasive existence of these dynamics in our home and work organisations. Garland (1998) describes how at different times in our lives we all unconsciously repeat and reverse past events, either directly or symbolically, in order to resolve internal conflicts. She also points out that the repetition and reversal in individuals who have not been traumatised is generally a more positive and creative activity than it is in traumatised individuals (*ibid.*). These repetitions and reversals shaped by our life experiences can influence the way we behave in our families, in groups and in our work organisations. Bion (1961) uses the term "valency" to describe the individual's tendency to relate and respond to groups and group processes in her own particular way. Developing an awareness of our own valency could help us identify our vulnerabilities towards certain projections and acting out, thus reducing the likelihood of the organisation's task being neglected or inadvertently perverted. The risk of jeopardising one's own psychological survival would also be minimised by increased self-awareness.

It is essential that systems for listening, thinking and containment (Bion, 1962; Garland, 1998) are built into organisations at all levels, allowing for the complex dynamics that manifest in organisations to be thought about and processed, and some ways forward identified. In addition, resources need to be spent on developing clinical staff, leaders and managers with the skills necessary to understand and work more effectively with trauma in these challenging environments (Adshead, 1998).

Conclusion

As a concept, trauma is a very useful way of understanding the pathology of forensic patients who have typically been both the victims and the perpetrators of traumatic events. The offence may be a re-enactment of their own trauma, whereby they have turned their position of helplessness and passivity into destructive action. In so doing, they may unconsciously be attempting to gain mastery over an earlier trauma, or to communicate what has happened to them in a primitive way. Treatment of trauma requires a theoretical framework. In the absence of a theoretical framework, there is a risk that within the institutional setting, traumatic acting out will be perpetuated rather than contained in a way that enables traumatised people to think about what has happened to them and what the impact has been on their lives and the lives of others.

Hospitalised forensic patients represent a particularly complex population from the perspective of trauma. This is because they may have experienced multiple types of trauma throughout their development. The impact of traumatic events is also determined by the nature of an individual's internal world of conscious and unconscious experiences of self and others. Those forensic patients who have experienced highly depriving, rejecting early carers are likely to present with disturbed personalities and ways of relating which ensure that the environment replicates their experiences through the relationships they have with carers and the relationships the carers have with each other. The effective management and treatment of groups of traumatised forensic patients in secure institutions may represent one of the last major clinical challenges forensic mental health nurses have to address in the literature and through research.

CHAPTER TWO

The dreaded and dreading patient and therapist

Carine Minne

What is it like to work psychoanalytically in a high-secure hospital setting with patients who dread treatment and who can provoke a sense of dread in their therapist? For a start, these patients would probably be the least likely to be considered suitable for a psychoanalytic approach. They have been violent physically to others and to themselves, show a phenomenal capacity to be violent to their own and others' minds, and are high homicide and/or suicide risks. Firstly I will give some background about working psychoanalytically in secure hospital settings with detained patients of this degree of disturbance. Secondly, in order to illustrate the sense of dread that arose in both patient and therapist, I will offer my attempts to work psychoanalytically with a very disturbed, suicidal young woman who killed her baby.

It is interesting that forensic psychiatry settings have embraced a psychoanalytic approach more than any other branch of psychiatry. An increasing appreciation has arisen of the impact on staff and on the organization of working with highly disturbed and disturbing patients. Institutions that house large numbers of such highly disturbed, violent patients could be considered to be chronically sick places that require chronic treatment themselves. This is reflected in many ways: high rates of sickness in staff, high turnover of staff, difficulties in recruiting, and all manner of staff-patient, patient-patient and manager-staff enactment of maladaptive scenarios on wards, in corridors and at clinical and administrative meetings. If we consider that many of these patients suffering from severe personality disorders and/or psychotic illnesses manifest their suffering through violent enactments, then it becomes clearer what the staff, particularly nurses, are exposed to on a daily basis and how the patients' disorders inevitably "spread" to the multidisciplinary teams and throughout the organization. A psychoanalytic perspective is essential in secure hospitals and units where the ingredients for institutional ill-health are potent and the personality disorders are, basically, contagious. Psychoanalytic input can provide a degree of immunity to this contagiousness through treatments, supervisions, consultations and training, but especially by bringing to attention the unconscious aspects.

Working psychoanalytically in such settings necessarily affects how we work, and adaptations have to be made. It is a frequent misperception that people in high-secure hospital conditions are referred to as prisoners. This is the familiar pull towards a custodial and punitive focus and away from the idea of treatment, often misconstrued by the general public as condoning the awful offences that have been committed. What is required is the right balance for each individual case between the provision of treatment by the mental health professionals on the one hand, and loss of freedom within a secure environment as required by the criminal justice system on the other. Both positions are essential for the proper care of any patient and the safety of the public. The difficulties in achieving this balance contribute to one of the particular dynamics when working under conditions of high security, where providing treatment and security can clash.

For example, all of us working in high security carry an enormous bunch of keys tied to our waists. Simply in terms of adding to the "them" versus "us" or "envious" versus "enviable" scenarios, the impact of this cannot be ignored. Here, straight away, a most concrete split is set up where patients and professionals are dressed in their respective costumes, ready to enact the familiar sado-masochistic script often apparent in places where so-called "bad" people are housed. Unless one remains constantly aware of this, one can fall for the magnetic pull of such transference and countertransference phenomena, and enact again and again the patients' internal worlds, which they can and do succeed in getting the professionals to sculpt with them.

Another difference from "general" psychotherapy is that within secure inpatient settings we go to see our patients rather than assuming that they are able to come and see us. Even if we had enough escort staff and rooms available, this expectation would place too much responsibility on many of our patients. Often a long time passes before a patient we see considers him- or herself to be a patient. Eventually, once back in the community after several years, some of these patients attend the Portman Clinic as outpatients, and this is quite a dramatic moment for them in their therapy if that change—from therapist going to see them to the patients coming to see their therapist—can occur.

Another consequence of working in a high-security environment is that the balance between confidentiality to our patients and the need to communicate information to the clinical team caring for them needs to be reviewed constantly. Regular discussions with colleagues are necessary, for example, in terms of anticipating and managing risk situations or addressing team splits that arise. In that sense, this work resembles child psychoanalytic treatments where some discussion with "parental" figures is necessary. Indeed, many of the patients could be considered at times as tiny babies or toddlers in adult bodies whose development had been severely interrupted when they were catastrophically damaged by unbelievably traumatic events at early stages in their lives.

The physical security of such treatment centres can appear sinister and inhibiting; in fact, provision of a necessary, firm, external boundary for these patients (who have often had no containment before) can offer them an opportunity to engage with treatment. A few of us are very much involved in providing long-term continuity of the psychoanalytic treatment across decreasing levels of security until the patient is back in the community, if this is feasible and ongoing treatment is recommended. This can provide the patients with the chance of continuing to work through the various transferential situations that arise during several years of treatment in the secure environment. Continuity is all the more important at times of transition, when anxieties are at their highest, regressed states of mind are common, and patients are at higher risk of acting out, in particular of suicidality. At these times, patients have to manage losing all previous, fragile, new attachments as well as a familiar environment as they move geographically to another unit and to a completely new team, often repeating their earlier experiences of a multitude of carers and homes. It can also be a terribly shaming thing for the patients to indicate anxiety about leaving and, even worse, to fail.

In the context of the preceding considerations regarding high-secure forensic settings, I will address treatment issues. A major task of this kind of treatment is to enable an awareness of the mind and its functions to become available to the owner of that mind, the person known to us as the patient. This refers to an awareness of who they, the patients, are, what they have done, and the impact of this on their minds and on the minds of others. Regardless of their diagnoses, people who have carried out serious violent offences, killing others as a way of killing parts of themselves, often have little or no awareness of themselves or of the seriousness of what they have done. This absence or avoidance, provided by an arsenal of psychotic and non-psychotic defences, appears to be necessary for the patient's psychic survival. Indeed, addressing their defences can cause massive anxieties about "cracking up" and can lead to psychotic breakdowns and, perhaps, to suicidality or even suicide. Yet to allow these defences to remain untouched can leave intact essential ingredients for being violent again. The therapist's task is a delicate and complicated one: (1) to help cultivate awareness in the patient's mind without seeming to commit a violent assault on that mind; (2) to judge clinically when such awareness is developing; and (3) to gauge continually in what way the patient is using his or her new awareness. These are the shifts we look for in monitoring our work. It is also these very shifts or, prognostically, positive internal world changes, that can provoke particular negative therapeutic responses which can become one source of dread in the therapist. In some cases, the careful and limited use of anti-psychotic medication can helpfully sedate the more intense psychotic anxieties and make ongoing psychoanalytic treatment possible.

I would now like to refer to how these patients are traumatised three-fold because this is so relevant to working psychotherapeutically with them. These patients are traumatised firstly by their appalling background histories, secondly by the offences they committed, and thirdly by their gradual discovery during treatment of having a mental disorder. Dr Leslie Sohn and I believe that this multiple traumatisation can lead in the course of treatment to a development and manifestation of a post-traumatic stress-type of disorder, which in our view should be seen as a positive prognostic indicator. In other words, as awareness and understanding develop, patients begin to suffer the consequences. Despite the distress which "getting better" causes, some of these patients can make tentative shifts towards a healthier internal world. However, as I have emphasized, precisely these shifts can provoke a particular negative therapeutic reaction, the aim of which is to try and return the patient's mind to its previous disturbed but familiar state—because a return to oblivion is more desirable than managing the burden of awareness.

I will now illustrate treatment dynamics in the case of a young woman whose prognosis is very poor and who could not maintain positive shifts. I have found her to be a much more difficult patient to see than all the very violent young men I also see. I have often dreaded going to her sessions and welcomed being "sacked" by her, which I was frequently. The staff team and I have had to work hard together to process the patient's regular provocations to re-enact her trauma in which she or we are like her mother. This trauma was reproduced both in her offence—she killed her own baby—and in her chronic suicidality, a state in which she is again identified with the mother who "killed" her. I have the informed consent of the patient and her psychiatrist's agreement to use anonymised case material from my work with her, which is discussed regularly with Dr Leslie Sohn and could not have been maintained without such consultations. I am also grateful to Dr Estela Welldon, whose work on the perversion of the maternal instinct (1992), as well as several private communications, has been invaluable.

Ms B is a 28-year-old woman who killed her nine-week-old daughter and later seriously wounded a professional. She comes from a large and highly dysfunctional family where trans-generational incestuous relationships have resulted in no one being sure of who is who in the extended family. Violence between different sets of parents, mother with father and mother with stepfathers, was the norm. There was no experience of consistent mothering. This young woman developed a tic disorder around puberty which was eventually treated with medication. She met a young man when she was 18 years old and made a conscious decision that he was the man with whom she would leave home, marry and have children. Prior to this she had no serious boyfriends, and one could speculate to what extent Ms B was attempting to undo some of the chaos in which she had been raised by having a "white wedding". Following their marriage, she and her husband lived together with his alcoholic mother.

Ms B was soon delighted to discover that she was pregnant. However, the stress of this event on such an ill-equipped young couple led to the breakdown of their marriage late in her pregnancy. She returned home to live with her own mother, but within days of Ms B delivering a healthy baby girl, her mother asked her to leave and go to live elsewhere because she could not stand the crying baby. This behaviour was quite typical of the mother, who later, for example, frequently told Ms B that she would be better off committing suicide than causing all this trouble. Ms B and her newborn baby subsequently moved in with a family friend.

Ms B developed concerns about her baby soon after she was born. She was convinced that the baby was sick and called her Health Visitor and General Practitioner on a regular basis, but she could never accept reassurance. On one occasion, she stated that the baby had started to manifest facial tics which were similar to her own and of such severity that the baby's breathing was affected. The mother and baby were admitted to hospital for the baby to be monitored. Initially, the baby was found to be well, but after two days the baby's condition began to deteriorate. No cause for this deterioration could be found. The baby became critically ill, needed to be looked after in intensive care, and then died.

Ms B, bereft, went home with her mother. Soon after the baby's death and post-mortem, laboratory reports showed toxic levels of Ms B's medication in the baby's blood that were considered to have caused the death by poisoning. She was arrested and charged with murdering her baby. In view of her fragile mental state, her remand period was spent in psychiatric hospital. She denied any wrongdoing for over a year until the end of the trial, when she admitted having given the baby her medication, not to kill the baby but out of concern that the doctors and nurses were not looking after the baby properly.

Retrospectively, it could be suggested that she had projected her own bad experience of being mothered twice over: once into her own baby by identifying with her mother, and then again by projective identification with the nurses and doctors, who became the bad parents for not noticing what was going on within the sick baby (herself) as well as the actual sick baby.

Ms B was finally convicted of infanticide and admitted to a locked ward under a hospital order from the court. Attempts were made gradually to give her increasing responsibility for herself with, eventually, short unescorted leave periods to her mother's home. Following an overnight home visit, she seriously attacked a nurse. The nurse was in the patient's room and had suggested that she begin thinking about taking down all the photographs of her baby in order to try and "move on". Perhaps the patient felt that she was being asked to give up her failed attempts to mourn, and this precipitated a catastrophe in her mind which could only be managed through a violent enactment due to an inability to "mind" it. Ms B was consequently transferred to high security and then began psychoanalytic psychotherapy.

During the first few months of treatment, she presented as a model, compliant patient who did as she imagined was expected of her in that situation—which is no more than one can expect from someone with such a history. She presented as a distressed patient who spoke about what a dreadful thing she had done, but all of this had a pseudo-feel to it. This way of presenting to me was gradually shown to her and interpreted as one way she had of avoiding feeling traumatised or victimised by her own disturbed state of mind, at the time of her offences and now in the room with me. This led to suicidality and a further increase in her dangerousness towards herself for a period of time.

In some sessions during these early months of therapy, she was more able to speak to me about what she did to her baby, how she crushed her tablets and secretly fed them to the baby, over and over again. Her real distress was very apparent. She described her preoccupation at the time with her belief that the baby was not being looked after properly by the nurses and doctors. I said to her, at these moments in her sessions, how she wished to be the baby that could be looked after properly. But such opportunities to feel understood trigger a highly ambivalent situation for this patient, for she is faced with the problem that to be looked after properly negates her view of what proper looking after means within her family structure and creates a sense of betraying her family if she follows the trend of her therapy. I therefore had to be kept as someone who was bound to harm her in some way, and her history and offence were once more re-enacted.

The pathological mother-child dynamic present in this patient's mind could also be seen in her therapy when, unbeknown to anyone, she took an overdose before a session and then came for her therapy, appearing with glazed eyes and bilateral hand tremor. She denied several times that anything was the matter when her physical state was commented on, became angry and shouted that there was no point in all this, and insisted that she wanted to be with her baby, another reference to her suicidality. She kept me in a concerned state and, after considering the likelihood of her having taken an overdose (because of a particular constellation of symptoms that became more apparent), I told her that I thought she wanted me to be a good mother and guess what the matter was. This was followed by a long silence. I then said that I believed she would be relieved if I guessed. I proceeded to tell her that I thought she wanted me to know that she had taken an overdose. If I did not notice this, then she could congratulate herself that she was right, no one notices she is serious (about suicide). If I did notice, she would get something from me but it would feel spoilt because of how she got it.

In this situation, the patient did finally admit to having taken an overdose, which then had to be dealt with medically as a matter of urgency. In this session the offence was repeated again: a baby (herself) was harmed with medication; but this time the baby was saved. Indeed, the "being saved" led to a manic outburst of profuse thanks from the patient, which diluted the seriousness of what had just happened and avoided the experience of guilt that such a saving could provoke.

In the first two years of treatment, Ms B's perception of me was of someone bound to harm her and, in that situation, trying to "poison" her with my words. She was frequently placed on continuous observation due to the episodes and threats of self-harm. On other occasions, which could last for several weeks or months, she would become manically freed from all her difficulties and claim to be cured and no longer in need of any treatment from anyone, especially from me. During these phases, she could become extremely hostile and even violent—indeed, she is the only patient for whom I have ever had to press the emergency alarm. For weeks at a time, I would absolutely dread going to her ward to see her because she would greet me with a seething, hostile, contempt, make personal remarks about my appearance and, following this, expose me to a relentless attack on my professional integrity which sometimes ended with threats of violence towards me. I was frequently "sacked" by the patient during these phases, which, to my shame, I welcomed.

Discussions with the nurses and regular consultations with Dr Sohn enabled me to keep thinking about what was going on and how important it was to remain available as a thoughtful, non-retaliatory and non-abandoning object, an experience she had never had before. Eventually, her "cured" state of mind would crumble when, once more, she would self-harm and enter a withdrawn and even less receptive state of mind. Breaks in therapy often triggered deteriorations in her mental state and the consequent need to increase her levels of observation due to the risk of self-harm. Any attempts to show her links between her feelings and the presence or absence of those around her were totally negated; the idea of being affected by such things was too frightening, impossible to "mentalize", and therefore only manifest in her behaviour. Contact with nursing staff was absolutely crucial throughout all these phases, especially given that my presence on the ward could cause major disruptions when all had been quiet and peaceful beforehand. The nurses were invaluable in enabling the therapy to be maintained during these difficult periods and in avoiding the temptation, present in therapist and nurses, to enact what was being provoked—a violent retaliation or a permanent rejection.

In the third year of treatment, Ms B's mental state deteriorated into a more overtly psychotic presentation when she appeared perplexed and had paranoid delusions of being poisoned by staff as well as experiencing hallucinations. She stopped eating and drinking and required transfer to the medical ward, where she seemed relieved and gratified at being tube fed, which she never refused, as though delegating her need to torture herself to those around her, including her therapist. This could also be understood as a regressed state where she was once more fused with the mother, albeit a sadistic, cruel one.

What emerged from this more psychotic presentation several months later was a patient who appeared depressed and who complained of flashbacks and nightmares, the content of these always being about her daughter's last hours attached to life-saving equipment and then in the morgue with a damaged dead body. Many sessions were brief, and consisted of the patient slowly shuffling into the room and reporting the following, with her head down, no eye contact, and in a monotonous voice: "I can't keep going like this. I want to be with my baby. I don't deserve to live. I don't deserve to die". Eventually she would ask a nurse to come and liberate her from me. I would try to take up with her how she mercilessly punished the baby's mother, herself. I would also take up with her how I was felt to be the punitive one, punishing the baby's mother. She was the baby as well, who was being harmed by me and needed to be rescued from me by the nurses.

There appeared to be a clash in Ms B's mind between the part that killed her baby, or herself, and knew it, colliding with the grieving part that experienced the flashbacks and longed to be an ordinary grieving mother or person. A basic struggle at this time in the therapy was whether she could face up to knowing who she was and what she had done, and therefore be able to change; or whether she needed to go back to, or stay in, a state of not knowing. In my view, there is a link between these positions in terms of her dangerousness. In the situation of remaining unaware, she remains a chronic risk to her babies, actual ones or symbolic representations of them. The pathological mother-child dynamic remains intact. In the situation of getting to know herself and being helped to deal with this knowledge, the risk to these babies diminishes, but without treatment or good risk management, the risk of dangerousness to herself rises. Both these dangerous attitudes could be considered suicidal, indirect or direct. In parallel with this conflict, Ms B fluctuated between three main states of being—distressed, withdrawn, experiencing flashbacks and self-harming; psychotic with delusions of being poisoned; or manically free of all problems, hostile towards carers and claiming to be "cured"—which continued over the following two years of treatment.

During the first five years of treatment, Ms B had two relationships with male patients. The first lasted for one year, after which the man was discharged, subsequently re-offended, was convicted of rape and attempted murder and incarcerated in prison. This was a particularly difficult time for Ms B as she attempted to address her pathological attachment to this man in his absence and to distance herself from him. Given her history of perceiving herself as betraying her family by behaving differently (decently), exploration of this relationship was extremely difficult for her. Her mother further complicated the situation by repeatedly telling her, when she broke off this relationship, that she should "stand by [her] man". Indeed, her mother began to visit this man in prison, which further confused the patient. Ms B subsequently began another relationship with a man in high security, whom she married whilst they were both still inpatients. This occurred during one of her phases of being manically "cured", and any attempts on my part to show her how she was repeating aspects of her troubled family history were to no avail. Indeed, in the context of a system that could be described as colluding with delusions of normality, psychotherapeutic work was rendered meaningless. He was also discharged, and they kept in contact at her mother's insistence; later on, Ms. B's mother had an affair with this man herself. Given this constellation, it is not difficult to see just how strongly the impact of Ms B's current situation, as well as that of her history, continues to jeopardise her chances of getting better.

After learning of the affair between her mother and her husband, Ms B managed to break off contact with her mother for over two years. She also began divorce proceedings. During this period of time, a more receptive involvement in her psychotherapy developed and her mental state was more stable. Her relationships with the nurses also improved, and there was just a glimpse of the beginning of change possible in her way of relating. In particular, Ms B seemed to be starting to give up her usual sado-masochistic way of relating with her "internal" mother, but this was only possible by simultaneously breaking off the relationship with the actual mother. However, her mother resumed contact with Ms B after the affair with that man ended. She told her daughter, my patient, that she should be grateful to her for saving her from being with such a terrible man. In an instant, the idealised image of her mother resurfaced in Ms B's mind and her therapist once more became the "bad" person (object) from whom only "poison" could be expected. Ms B's incipient progress was halted in its tracks. This development was a further clear indication to me and the team that contact with her mother was truly detrimental to her mental health; and if she had been a child (which she is emotionally but not in real terms), child protection laws could have been invoked to prevent contact with the mother for the sake of the well-being of that child.

Unfortunately, the patient has remained stuck, and now often somatizes her unbearable mental experiences or risks developing overt psychotic symptoms. Both these positions prevent her from being able to engage in a dialogue about the contents of her mind with her therapist. She has also maintained the idealised mother in her mind, with the implication that the pathological and dangerous mother-child dynamic remains. The reason for Ms B's lack of sustained progress is most likely due to a damaged mental structure leaving her unable to maintain or further develop the initial shift to healthier relating of which we only caught glimpses. The main responses in therapist and staff are hopelessness or fury, both of which are of course prominent within the patient. Interestingly, the main responses towards Ms B by other patients vary between hostile hatred towards her when she is at her most suicidal and despairing and, on the other hand, ignoring her when she is in her manically "cured" states. Evoking such negative and neglectful reactions guarantees that Ms B will feel "mother's" presence even on the ward.

It is very likely that Ms B will require permanent institutional care. The psychoanalytic input has perhaps not ameliorated her situation, but it has at least helped her carers to understand her and to keep trying to give meaning to her life as it has been and continues to be. A therapist/object who is able, with the help of nursing staff, to tolerate the spectrum of mental states with which she presents and not retaliate or run away may also contribute something to her internal world which may only become apparent in later years.

Conclusion

One aim in providing this kind of input is to enable the nurses to carry out their difficult task of being the recipients of powerful projections and to manage the other patients who, likewise, are deeply affected by each other. Another aim in providing therapy to patients like this, as part of the overall treatment, is to attempt to bring about a gradual realisation within themselves regarding what they have done and what kind of mental life they had lived before that allowed these awful events. These previous mental lives or mental states are those which the patients resume when in regressed states. The process of treatment appears to require a complicated and lengthy transition period from not knowing anything about themselves to becoming more aware and dealing with the consequent profoundly traumatic effects. The objective is to help them gain understanding and, optimistically, some change in their internal worlds. This may involve a change from a more pathologically defended personality disordered or psychotic presentation to one reminiscent of a post-traumatic stress disorder type of presentation. If such a change can take place, patients might feel much worse at first, but they would have a healthier internal world where thoughts and feelings about what happened, as well as their predicament in relation to this, could be experienced in the mind without the need to get rid of their mental experiences in the familiar way of acting them out violently.

As these patients make progress with treatment, a major difficulty arises when a particular negative therapeutic reaction—provoked by "getting better"—supervenes. With consistency over a long period of time, it is possible for these patients to make tentative shifts towards the "depressive position", and this is something that needs to be worked through over and over again, until the negative therapeutic responses triggered by the positive shifts lessen in severity and frequency. How much further one can go in Ms B's particular case remains a question. Her capacity for self-reflection is limited from developmental damage sustained. Her ability to regulate her affects is seriously impeded and leads to impulsive, violent behaviour. Her main defence mechanisms are primitive and have been seen to be stable but inflexible. Her mind is populated with objects that devalue or punish, and this leads to a dependence on external others onto whom she projects her distorted view of them as good or bad. Ms B's central fears revolve around the eternally intrusive presence of the bad object or, just as awful, the always impending loss of the good one she never quite had. These chronic dreads fuel her suicidal and self-harming tendencies.

Long-term continuity of treatment, throughout patients' transitions to different levels of security, is necessary to enable real shifts to arise, with the hope that the muscles of the mind strengthen and can tolerate and contain what previously needed to spill out of the mind into bodily action. It is a lot to ask of people who suffer the triple traumas described earlier, as well as being a lot to ask of those caring for and those sharing a home with them; but we feel committed to offering the treatment they so desperately need and so desperately dread.

CHAPTER THREE

X-treme group analysis: on the countertransference edge in inpatient work with forensic patients

John Gordon, Sharman Harding, Claire Miller and Kiriakos Xenitidis

Introduction

For group analysts and many other professionals, the work of Murray Cox (Cordess & Cox, 1996 for bibliography) is an abiding influence and inspiration. When clinical encounters unfold within the locked setting with patients whose treatment orders are characterized by a phrase Cox often used, "without limit of time" (Cox, 1978, p. 14), dilemmas totally different even from forensic outpatient therapy must be considered. Establishing analytic groups on secure inpatient wards is a complicated process. Careful and often protracted preliminary attention to negotiating with managers and consultant psychiatrists, liaising with multidisciplinary teams, identifying and evaluating patients, finding a time and a room for the group, and navigating against and within the unconscious collective dynamics of the organization—the social defence system (Jaques, 1955; Menzies, 1960) are all extremely arduous, frustrating and important.

Furthermore, the potential conflicts between a voluntary, confidential, humane endeavour such as dynamic psychotherapy and the social/institutional imperatives of security and risk assessment have led Pilgrim (1988, 1997), for example, to conclude that the offer of psychotherapy comes close to mystification by evading the all-pervasive reality of social control: "If hospitals are functioning as prisons and diagnosis is glossing a process of indefinite detention, it is necessary that such relationships are exposed for what they are. Such an exposure will probably lead to the conclusion that much of our present secure provision requires dismantling, rather than that such provision should deploy more psychotherapy" (1988, p. 69). Our approach highlights difficulties different from the political/sociological ones elaborated by Pilgrim. Although we agree with the general perspective of systems theory, according to which organizations, their manifest tasks and their implicit functioning must be considered in relation to their external (social, political, legal and cultural) environment (Obholzer & Roberts, 1994; Hirschhorn, 1995), it is vital to recognize that Pilgrim's stark dichotomy at the social level—control versus diagnosis/treatment—risks oversimplifying a more complex and confusing psycho-social reality.

For example, a frequent and very disconcerting occurrence on secure wards is that patients who complain bitterly and eloquently about being locked up, assiduously consult their solicitors, and demand that the (escorted or unescorted) leave due them is provided punctiliously by nursing staff (whenever the patient wants it and for as long, to the minute, as is formally specified), break down when discharge beckons. This occurs so regularly with some patients that, after a number of years, staff speak openly of a pattern. "Institutionalization" was the term coined decades ago to designate the repetitive dismantling within custodial organizations of inmates' social skills and capacities through total control and induction of dependence. However, psychoanalytic study of institutionalization revealed ubiquitous systematic and unconscious mutual pressures between staff and inmate/patient sub-groups which powerfully affected the experiences of each: experiences of the organization itself and of the identities of self and other (Main, 1989; Hinshelwood, 1998).

In secure forensic settings we find to an extraordinary degree patients who exemplify Lucas' reminder that "the commonest presenting symptom of psychosis is not hallucinations or delusions, which are found in some 60% of cases, but lack of insight presenting as denial and rationalization, which is found in over 90% of cases" (2003, p. 36). And unlike psychotic patients in general, forensic patients have enacted their impulses, often catastrophically, and so combine denial with radical loss of control. It is understandable that someone who has committed an irreparable action needs to obliterate any capacity to be aware of what has happened—and of what might be repeated—although without awareness and self-knowledge, the chances of repetition are much increased. When the personality carries out such "mental surgery" on itself, the removal of self-awareness only exacerbates the already-excised self-control. But since "mental surgery" is a psychological phantasy and not a medical specialty, what happens to the patient's self-reflective awareness and self-control? However rudimentary or damaged, they cannot disappear into thin air.

We believe that these capacities and functions are reallocated, attributed and stirred up in members of the staff sub-group within the organization. Through constant emotional interactions between patients and staff, the intolerably painful and persecuting abilities to monitor and control, as they are decreasingly exercised by patients on themselves, seem—to both patients and staff—to be exclusively deployed by staff. On the one hand, there is nothing surprising about this, for after all, the staff role includes precisely the functions of observation and boundary regulation. Yet an unexpected result of this process of micro-institutionalization at an unconscious level is that the imprisoning quality mentioned by Pilgrim, and particularly the potentially intrusive and suffocating aspects of the patients' severely guilty self-awareness, are experienced by patients as emanating entirely from staff. And staff members, to their extreme dismay, begin to experience themselves as harsh, sometimes inhuman persecutors; or, cracking under the strain arising from the condemnations of their own guilty consciences as well as from the sometimes painful, sometimes threatening cries of the "victimized" patients, they wonder how they can justify their calling as caring professionals. Or alternatively, staff may spare themselves the anguish by relishing the position of dominating control on the basis that forensic inpatients are dangerous patients (Doctor, 2003; Gordon, 2004). Or the experience leaves staff feeling perplexed, anxious and sometimes deeply disturbed. These developments are much more insidious and complex than Pilgrim's dichotomy implies: control and diagnosis are not discrete, either-or options.

These are not simply theoretical considerations. A young female nurse, who does not usually work on the ward, walks down a long corridor with patients' rooms on either side. It is a winter evening so the light is subdued. As she passes a patient seated on a small couch near the end of the corridor, the patient takes his penis out of his trousers. She is stunned and upset as he watches her, and she quickly returns to the nursing station. Subsequently the ward manager addresses this issue with the patient, who denies utterly that it happened and rebukes the manager for hostile intentions to control the patient and ruin his opportunity for discharge. We can speculate about the degree of denial involved: does the patient really believe he did not act as observed by the nurse, or is his denial merely public, a lie? In either case, he is involved in attempting to substantially alter the awareness of his action, which has been located in the nurse and then attacked. The patient's evident inability to bring to bear appropriate controls on his impulses evokes the need for control in the ward manager. Both the awareness and the control, wiped out within the patient's personality, continue to be assaulted when they appear in the staff.

Or consider a much more frequent, less overtly perverse, even normal example which is ingrained in the everyday ward interactions between patients and nurses. At night, staff are required to check on sleeping patients at intervals to make sure they are all right. Patients are asked to leave the internal curtain on their doors half open to facilitate this observation, so that the nurse can open the external curtain and view the patient as tactfully as possible. However, many patients do not keep the internal curtain open, and staff must therefore enter the room. They then complain that staff constantly wake them up. Another variant of this quandary occurs, even if internal curtains are not closed, when staff find patients completely submerged in blankets, and are unable to detect if they are breathing. This may also require entry; but in order to prevent this if possible, staff will often shine a torch through the window for several minutes, which may disturb the patient. There is no way out of this inherent control-observation/care-diagnosis predicament, and concerned staff members must endeavour to cope with their own responses to the realization that caring may disturb and that paying attention may be experienced as sadistic control.

Of course group analysts also operate within the total organizational matrix, and are consequently subjected to and contribute to the dynamics of identity construction (Hinshelwood, 1989; Gordon, 1999) which have been described in the preceding vignettes. Once analytic groups are established, clinical work must confront the extreme pressures which emotional contact with forensic inpatients place on the countertransference. To put it bluntly, after an initial phase of group analysts' anxiety mixed with excitement and concomitant idealization of the supervisor, it becomes virtually impossible to work analytically with forensic patients because of the countertransference. For prolonged periods, therefore, the countertransference must be sustained, contained and explored. To do this means that supervision—the "*sine qua non* of all forensic undertakings" (Cox, 1996, p. 199)—becomes a thoroughly persecutory experience, an arena of delimited but frankly paranoid (psychotic) transferences to the supervisor. Such a development is intolerable, annihilates workgroup functioning, but cannot be avoided. Its phenomena include (1) total thought block; (2) ideas of reference; (3) rage; (4) disintegration of professional, and occasionally personal, identity; (5) mute silence; (6) profound shame and guilt over manifest incapacity, alternating with (7) grandiosity and feelings of entitlement; and (8) breaking of boundaries. These are marks of the psychic assaults referred to in the title of this book, and they inevitably occur, no matter how highly trained the professionals.

No one who is aware of the "parallel process" between clinical session and supervision should be surprised at such extreme states of mind evinced by group analysts, which dramatically reflect the transference impacts of patients' severe psychopathology. But it is the case that some accounts of work with forensic patients in group analysis, particularly when detailed clinical material from group sessions is mentioned, give scant or rather general attention to countertransference (Schlapobersky, 1996; Welldon, 1984, 1993, 1997). Welldon does note the primitive, highly sexualized enactments within outpatient groups, but she does not refer explicitly to the group analyst's emotional responses (1984). It could be inferred that they mirror those recognized in other group members who, for example, feel seduced and intensely excited by a group member's perversion. There are references to the "dynamite" qualities of patient-therapist contact and to how personal therapy and institutional structures should protect therapists from "the inherent anxiety produced by working with forensic patients" (Welldon, 1993, p. 493). Nevertheless, the group analyst in action, if not the forensic student (Welldon, 1996), tends to be represented as poised, aware, accepting, able to think and to communicate: an unruffled, "Foulkesian" image. We aim to fill in the countertransference picture by first reviewing relevant psychoanalytic clinical theory, and then trying to convey what it feels like to do group analysis on the edge.

Psychopathology and countertransference—intensifying responses

This section is theoretical and aims to clarify the reasons for such extreme emotional responses in group analysts during supervision. We will survey conceptualizations of the countertransference at increasingly serious levels of mental pain and illness. Clinical work with forensic patients involves not simply a summation of these levels, but a condensation and exponential escalation of transference pressure and countertransference resonance.

Freud's earliest statement regarding countertransference came in his address to the Nuremberg Congress in 1910, subsequently published as "The Future Prospects of Psycho-analytic Therapy" (Etchegoyen, 1991, p. 259; Freud, 1910). His formulation is that countertransference is the analyst's transference to the patient or to the work of analyzing. And notwithstanding all the subsequent elucidation of the concept, this "strict" or "narrow" definition remains the bedrock in work with forensic patients. (The "broad" connotation of the term is discussed below.)

> We have begun to consider the "counter-transference", which arises in the physician as a result of the patient's influence on his unconscious feelings, and we are almost inclined to insist that he shall recognize this counter-transference in himself and overcome it . . . we have noticed that no psycho-analyst goes further than his own complexes and internal resistances permit; and we consequently require that he shall begin his activity with a self-analysis and continually carry it deeper while he is making his observations on his patients. [Freud, 1910, p. 144–145]

Within two years, the capacity for self-analysis itself was viewed as emerging from and dependent on a training analysis, "laying oneself open to another person" (Freud, 1912, p. 116) in order to explore "complexes and resistances" which skew the relationship to the patient and may block contact and understanding. Freud was working with patients whom he considered as suffering from neurotic psychopathology: hysteria and obsessional states. His position is basically that restated years later by Money-Kyrle: "Now, to a parent, a child stands, at least in part, for an early aspect of the self. And this seems to me important. For it is just because the analyst can recognize his early self, which has already been analysed, in the patient, that he can analyse the patient" (1956, p. 360). Being in touch with the patient requires being in touch with similar fixations, defences, impulses, phantasies and conflicts in oneself. Otherwise, countertransference as resistance is inevitable because the analyst is blinded or counter-transfers his complexes onto the patient. McCarthy (1988), in a variation on this theme, wondered if incest victims were hated because their acting out of oedipal wishes was unacceptable to public and therapist alike.

How is it possible, sitting with a murderer, a sadistic paedophile, a rapist—or in an analytic group with them all—to find, let alone to convey an emotional understanding of such psychopathology in oneself? One way is to "bracket" the index offence in order to "get to know the patient as a person". This may lead to a deep identification with the traumatized, shamed child victim within the perpetrator (De Zulueta, 1993; Gilligan, 2000). But in order for such an identification to be analytically useful rather than a defensive splitting, disgust, hatred, dread and rejection (among many other emotional reactions) must be faced.

In the Introduction to this book an example is given of a nurse in a reflective practice group who spoke in increasingly open terms about his revulsion when he entered the staff toilet on the ward and saw it smeared with shit. When he began to elaborate his thoughts and feelings about the effects of this on female staff members and referred to an abhorrent image in his mind involving a patient and his own wife, the group members felt "grossed out", expostulated that he was going too far, and shut him up. Contact with the patient within his mind was threatening to blow this man's mind, but he had captured specific emotional experiences and was conveying them to his colleagues. They could not tolerate this. The group analyst felt half identified with the unanimous "shut up", half aware that real communication about the work was going on, but he was unable to intervene due to the paralyzing effects even of contact with a patient at one remove through the mind of the staff member. This basic countertransference, the worker's own intense emotional reaction to patients, can *on its own* render further contact and understanding impossible.

In regard to psychoanalytic psychotherapy with severe personality disorders, Kernberg wrote:

> Perhaps the most difficult aspect of the therapeutic interaction is the therapist's subjective experience as a reflection of a projected aspect of his patient's self experience . . . to tolerate what the patient, by means of projective identification, induces in him while the patient enacts the experience of his object representation. It is usually less difficult to tolerate the interaction when the therapist represents the patient's object representation directly. Insofar as the patient usually sees himself as the victim of a frustrating, overwhelming, unavailable, or sadistic object, identification with the patient's self-image at such points may threaten the therapist's ability to contain that reaction . . . and use it . . . in helping the patient transform action into subjective experience. [1984, p. 146]

Several points are evident from this formulation of countertransference with more disturbed patients. First, Kernberg uses the "broad" definition of countertransference: any and all physical, emotional and cognitive reactions of the analyst may reflect a facet of the patient's unconscious internal experience of himself relating to an object (another person). However much these responses are the analyst's and no one else's, the patient may have played a part—whether subtle and hard to recognize or blatant—in contributing to them. Countertransference is a counter-response to the patient's transference repetitions during which the patient may identify with himself or a significant object in interaction while casting the analyst in either one of these roles.

Second, the concept of projective identification is central in trying to understand both the means by which the patient repeats his internal world and the induced impacts on the receptive clinician. Projective identification is an unconscious phantasy (conviction) that in order to protect oneself from feared and hated feelings, thoughts, experiences or attributes, or to preserve valuable qualities which are believed to be at risk of loss or damage from destructive aspects within oneself, "mental surgery" can be performed on one's personality by oneself. Originally Klein (1946) considered this to be an internal operation which affected the way an individual came to experience and perceive himself and others in his own mind (a more concrete version of what Kernberg refers to as self and object representations). From the 1950s many psychoanalysts studied how such transformations of identity within the personality tended to be externalized and lived out with people in the patient's environment. Racker (1968), Heimann (1950), Bion (1961, 1984), Segal (1977), Ogden (1983), Pick (1985), Rosenfeld (1987) and Joseph (1989) in particular have studied the clinical interaction in minute detail to trace how such externalizations can totally envelop relationships between the patient and current significant people, things or places (objects) in his life.

Their findings add complexity to Freud's original concept of countertransference as comprising primarily the analyst's own problems and conflicts. The patient may projectively identify into the analyst's basic countertransference by, for example, making use of a pre-existing condemning attitude in the analyst's transference to his forensic patient in order to externalize a vindictive "object representation" which internally prosecutes the patient. Even unexpected or uncharacteristic feelings may suddenly be experienced full-force by staff members and, as Bion noted, are often believed to be "quite adequately justified by the objective situation without recourse to recondite explanation of their origin" (1961, p. 149).

Third, when the "recondite explanation" of countertransference murderousness amounts to a group of forensic personality disordered patients evacuating, "identijec[ting]" (Bion, 1992, p. 353) into their group analyst to maintain psychic equilibrium, the salience of Kernberg's remarks becomes all too evident.

Finally, contact with forensic cases leaves little doubt that it is as difficult to tolerate projective enactment of (and introjective identification with) object representations as it is of self-images. Internal objects can be unimaginably violent, and unless one adopts

Winnicott's concept of "objective hate in the countertransference" (1949), which we believe would be defensive, the experience of feeling taken over by violent urges towards the patient can be even worse than masochistic identification with the victim self.

From a clinical perspective, Hinshelwood (1999) calls attention to just such a problem in the countertransference with personality disordered patients who relentlessly attempt to rid themselves of a smothering, abusively violent internal object. And from a theoretical perspective on narcissistic personality disorders, Britton (2003) traces the development of the concept of the "ego-destructive superego" from Fairbairn's "internal saboteur", Freud's description of the melancholic's mercilessly destructive, sadistic superego, Klein's emphasis that "*love is necessary for survival*" (p. 120) in the face of a murderous internal object, to Bion's delineation in "Attacks on Linking" (1959) of a hypertrophied, super-superego dedicated to self-mutilation and annihilation of creativity. Britton further cites Darwin's fear of "crucifixion" when he contemplated sharing his ideas with senior colleagues (2003, p. 117) and suggests Marlowe's Tamburlaine—"an apparently conscienceless killer"—as an apt image of the "unreconstructed superego" (*ibid.*, p. 120). Projective pressures usually lead to alternating, even kaleidoscopic identifications in the countertransference with both self and object poles of forensic patients' internal "Tamburlaine" scenarios.

Many forensic patients have a dual diagnosis (personality disorder and psychosis, for example), while some of our patients in addition have long histories of substance abuse. Turning to this even more serious level of psychopathology, Robbins (1993) uses his unparallelled experience of psychoanalytic psychotherapy with schizophrenic and other psychotic patients to examine countertransference extensively at both individual and ward/institutional levels:

> Experienced therapists of psychosis ... believe that in the process of treatment the schizophrenic attempts to drive the analyst crazy. I look upon this elaboration of the psychoanalytic concepts of transference and countertransference as one of the more profound contributions to our understanding of therapy with schizophrenics ... and I think that many therapists who work with schizophrenics experience

> encapsulated psychoses in the relationship for greater or lesser periods of time. [p. 225]

Many other attempts to convey the quality of the psychotic transference-countertransference also focus on the cumulative impact of enacted meaninglessness (Hinshelwood, 1999, 2004), assaults on the capacity to generate meaning (Ogden, 1980), occupying "a non-position in the null dimension" (Eigen, 1985, p. 323), and attacks on linking (Bion, 1959). It is particularly difficult for a professional whose whole raison d'être is to find meaning to be on the receiving end of, and—maybe worse—to discover that the patient experiences him as, just such a negating spirit. When in addition to the psychotic transference the patient is known to have replaced symbol with catastrophic action, the countertransference is under maximum strain.

Robbins attends to countertransference at the macro level in a section called "The Matrix of Hospital Treatment":

> Working productively with schizophrenia involves the containment and channeling of rage ... So staff have an understandable stake in maintaining patients in the compliant, affectless, zombie-like (tranquillized) state that ensues when the adaptation related to the psychotic core becomes chronic, rather than allowing them to become actively affectively aroused and troublesome ... Hospital staff are ... by the nature of their roles perhaps even primed to enact a primary object countertransference with the schizophrenic patient which is qualitatively similar to the collusive countertransference of the therapist ... [and to] forces that are unconsciously enacted in various ways by all parties—patient, family, staff, and therapist ... [1993, p. 279]

Our analytic groups are inserted into this emotional force field, fundamental aspects of which include the individual and group-structured countertransference reactions whose features Robbins describes. We think of this as the social countertransference system and will now illustrate how we contribute to and struggle within it.

Clinical material: the group analyst's account

Seven male patients, a male group analyst and a female co-therapist from the ward make up this group. A, a middle aged man diagnosed with paranoid schizophrenia and a long history of alcohol abuse, has an index offence of manslaughter. B, of similar age, is schizophrenic, abuses alcohol and killed his child. C, also middle aged, suffers from a psychotic illness, misuses drugs and committed grievous bodily harm (GBH). D, slightly older, has a history of alcohol abuse, pathological jealousy, and a conviction for manslaughter. E and F, both some years younger, committed GBH and murder respectively, and abuse drugs. The considerably younger G is diagnosed with psychotic illness, abuses drugs and alcohol, and was convicted of arson.

Attendance is excellent, with full groups for about 70% of the time, probably due to the fact that this analytic group is part of a one-year highly structured group programme for non-acute patients referred from other wards to deal with their substance abuse. Several other (didactic) groups run concurrently.

The early phase of the group was dominated by themes of football, the club scene and DJ-ing. Prison and drug culture jargon were used in an attempt to exclude the therapists and register the group's resistance to participating in yet another "therapeutic" experience (Hinshelwood, 1997). The manifest regular attendance and apparent obedient participation was the "tip of the iceberg". The only stranger in the group was the group analyst, who was persistently interrogated over a number of sessions. Questions about his ethnic and religious background, food preferences, favourite mode of transport, etc., were repeated especially by D and C. As no satisfactory answers were received, a degree of covert hostility was developed as a response to a widely felt lack of trust and paranoia. "Never trust anybody in prison," said D, "especially when they offer you Maltesers" (chocolate balls). In terms of the countertransference this aggressive questioning and ongoing rivalry elicited a defensive response in the therapists and a realisation of the potential for violence in this at times sadistic group.

The middle phase was characterised by a degree of self-disclosure by most members and the absence of the co-therapist for personal and organizational reasons. E often talked about his psychotic experiences (hallucinations and delusions), with other members making connections with psychedelic drug-taking. He referred to how he had stabbed a stranger in the street under the influence of drugs and expressed remorse. Further, E mentioned his two teenage children whom he had never seen. A hardly ever talked in the group; when he did, covert hostility from the others was evident. D, a high-secure hospital and prison veteran, took pleasure in telling the group stories of the famous gangsters and other criminals he had met; he considered a missed session as a welcome break from the group.

The final phase was marked by the introduction of a second female co-therapist after it had become clear that the first could not continue. Many group members looked forward to the pending "conditional" discharge they expected. There was a recurrent theme of freedom, escape, discharge and ambivalence about discharge. G said that he had been told he would have to repeat the programme, but at least he had been granted "town leave" and could visit his mother. He had not been out for a year. The group analyst said that G was pleased but anxious going out, and G agreed. E announced happily that he had a pleasant surprise, great news: he was moving on soon to a rehab flat, but he was not sure exactly when. F, D and C were waiting for hostel vacancies. G felt left out; there was a sense of inequality and unfairness.

By the time the group ended after a symbolic nine months, the group analyst was no longer feeling a stranger. The first anniversary of September 11 triggered themes of extreme violence, mass loss of life and widespread anti-American sentiment. The group analyst commented that they were talking about how freedom is wasted by some people out there as they take it for granted. The conviction that lack of freedom leads to death came up repeatedly. D was watching with a degree of sadistic pleasure some pigeons becoming trapped between the building and a "safety net" just outside the group room. He commented that there will be a "carpet" of dead pigeons there the next day—a grim reminder of the dangerousness that needs to be contained (Doctor, 2003). Out of the blue, F asked the group analyst if he went to museums and stuff. The group analyst asked if he did, and C and D said they had. D made it very clear that "going to museums" meant wandering the streets. Covert (or not so covert) hostility towards the therapists was manifested in many forms. On one occasion, C said that the psychiatrists want to hear such things as "I was ill . . . it wasn't my fault", implying that one should lie in order to gain freedom. When D found out that the co-therapist drove a car, he said: "Oh dear, women will be voting next." On another occasion he sarcastically asked the analyst if he was paid for last week's (missed) session.

Supervisor's comments

The atmosphere of extreme threat and incipient violence was marked in this group from the beginning. Countertransference pressures on the group analyst were increased because of the inconsistent presence of the co-therapist, who was, however, very helpful at the start of the group. Very intrusive questioning of the group analyst contributed to his sense, regularly conveyed in supervision, of being under chronic siege. Occasionally he did resort to answering questions—for example, that he did not particularly like football—to try to stop the relentless pursuit. This climaxed with the Malteser image.

In supervision, a more complete version of the story was that D, a patient with a severe personality disorder who had "ruled" his prison and high-secure ward, frequently spoke in a friendly, joking manner. The Malteser material indelibly revealed the underlying sadistic violence in his "humour". A Malteser is offered to new prisoners as an apparent welcoming gift from the "old group" members, a "sweet" invitation to join the gang. In fact it is a small ball of shit rolled up to look like chocolate. A more cogent symbol of the violent evacuation of hostile and debased internal objects and agglomerated self components would be hard to imagine. Once inside the recipient, this murderously envious component wreaks secret havoc. The trapped, soon dead carpet of pigeons was seen as representing the defeated therapists at the triumphant end of the sessions. They no longer felt strangers, but such "acceptance" may indicate the relief of the Malteser consumer, terrified and alone in an unsafe and unfamiliar place, desperately relieved at signs of a "friendly welcome" and unaware of the damage being carried out from inside.

As portrayed by Susskind (1994) in his novel *Perfume*, the forensic *modus operandi* is destructive insinuation into the object enviously to extract and relish its coveted essence. The group analyst was in touch with the impacts of his patients; the consequent intense anxiety and paralysis of thought and communication—while retaining the capacity to observe—took courage and resilience to bear. An interpretation that the overwhelming curiosity (Bion [1957, 1958] considers such curiosity a feature of the psychotic part of the personality) reflected the patients' perception of the group analyst as tricky, manipulative and offering a Malteser in the form of "therapy" could only gradually be formulated from the distance of the supervisory session. C alludes to the issue when lies are promulgated as the best strategy for dealing with authority in this secure setting. The truth-telling of group analysis can be trapped subtly in nets and infused with poisoned shit.

This material calls to mind another image, that of the stool pigeon. A stool pigeon is used as a decoy to draw others into a net, hence the person used as a decoy for others; alternatively it is a police spy or informer. To speak the truth in a forensic analytic group can be experienced unconsciously as informing on oneself or others to the group analyst/police. The group analyst can also be perceived as a decoy, seducing information out of the patients which will be given to psychiatrists and the Home Office; in turn patients decoy the group analyst into believing they are telling the truth. When the transference-countertransference relationship is structured around a stool pigeon/Malteser dynamic, the group analyst is truly working on the edge.

Clinical material: the co-therapists' account

The session described comprises a group of male schizophrenic offender patients who are on a long-stay ward, and took place approximately eighteen months after the group commenced. Five patients attended this session.

A spoke with consternation about pressure. He was clearly anxious and very agitated, and demanded that the group analyst tell the doctors and nurses that he needed to go to the pub, he was sick of not feeling trusted. He said that he would only have 5% alcohol or half a pint, but gradually, as his agitation increased, he arrived at the point of wanting to get blasted. B interjected and said that he understood A and knew where he was coming from. C said, "Oh come on A, what are you getting at? You know what happens when you go outside: you get blasted and lose it." D said, "It's the pressure, man—nobody knows, nobody knows."

The group analyst spoke about the dilemma of wanting to be understood and trusted, yet also wanting to rebel and get into a state of mind which meant a loss of control and an escape from reality. E responded angrily, "Oh, HRH has the answers and I'm bloody sick of it." E then walked towards the door, and the co-therapist suggested that he stay as the issues expressed were important. E mumbled, "Oh all right, we are all just a group of clones." B asked what a clone was, and E replied, "Oh you know, we look the same, the same imprints." E glared at the group analyst and said, "Can you see any differences?" At this point E mumbled in disdain and left the room.

The co-therapists were left feeling rather insignificant and useless. Communications from the patients came in the form of floods, and any links made by the therapists were rubbished and rejected. The co-therapist spoke about identity and feelings related to being a patient which were hard to manage.

A asked if he could leave, as he needed to make a telephone call. The co-therapist replied that it was important for him to stay in the group. A said he did not have anything more to say, and left. After a few minutes, E returned with a cup of tea. C asked E why he had talked about clones, and E replied, "Well, when the psychoanalysts speak, they know the answers, it's not any help really. A clone is just a cardboard cut-out."

The group analyst spoke about the idea of a cardboard cut-out being like a mask where the identity was concealed, and added that wearing a mask covered up the true identity, which may represent a form of protection or a way of avoiding feelings of vulnerability. C said, "We are all vulnerable. It's difficult to feel exposed." D, who had been sitting quietly, was wearing sunglasses and a top hat in which he had tucked his dreadlocks. E, laughing, asked D why he was dressed up. D said that the lights were too bright, they were "piercing, piercing, going inside". The group analyst commented that he may be feeling under the spotlight in the group, and also wary of being seen. D then removed his shades and beamed, saying, "It's about vanity, my friend. It's about vanity." D then said E looked good with his new haircut. E had had his head shaved, which made him look more intimidating. D and E interacted in a jokey way, and after a few minutes D removed his top hat, released his dreadlocks, and replaced his hat.

In this session the patients were communicating feelings relating to frustration, tensions and the loss of identity. The therapists struggled to make connections and links with the patients, who avoided contact and defended against their vulnerability. Some group members showed signs of great resistance to the therapeutic process: when links were made these patients either left the room or dismissed any therapeutic interventions. There was also an ability in two patients, C and D, to demonstrate the feeling of being understood and to make bridges either by words or by actions. The states of mind of these patients constantly oscillate between reality and non-reality. The group described here, who seek contact yet also fear it, constantly challenge the therapeutic process. This paradox leaves the therapists feeling attacked, useless and unable to think, which can be very painful.

Supervisor's comments

Just as secondary revision of a dream lends narrative structure, coherence and clarity to a form of thinking which is obscure, confused and resists contained representation, so the above account struggles to render comprehensible the core experience of being and working under the piercing pressure which characterises this analytic group. The prospect of making contact with blasting (with beta elements fit only for evacuation [Bion, 1962]) and blasted minds is formidable. A key feature which is not directly mentioned, but like the latent dream is elusively present in E's scathing HRH remark, is that both group analyst and co-therapist are women. HRH is Her Royal Highness, a term which alternates with explicit use of denigrating and abusive "sexual" images; the co-therapist is given nicknames which seem to reflect the status of a maid to HRH. The clothes worn by the therapists are subjected to close scrutiny and commentary of a very intrusive kind by group members, some of whom have committed sexual assaults. When the co-therapists refer to issues of threatened identity, vulnerability, self-protection and unmanageable feelings, it is clear that they are not only referring to the patients—although the interventions are addressed to the latter.

In supervision, the full extent of the turmoil evoked by emotional contact with these patients emerges. A projective system is being enacted in the session in which patients expel under pressure their intolerable tensions, and the co-therapists, through reciprocal attributive projective identification (Britton, 2003), perceive themselves as seeking contact and the patients as resisting and attacking therapeutic work. The clones and cardboard cut-outs are reflections of the resultant state in which every personality is flattened and hidden in the "null dimension" (Eigen, 1985, p. 323). "It is important to stay in the group," the patients are told; the capacity of the co-therapists to sustain their observations on the piercing countertransference edge is even more vital. Insight into the countertransference began to emerge in a much later supervision, when clear relief at E's departure from the group room could be acknowledged at the same moment as he was being told that he should try to stay in the session. We could then begin to wonder about the internal and external object who longs for contact and is deeply relieved to be free of it without clone-creating wholesale mutual projections.

Conclusion: reflective practice—the group analyst's work with the ward staff

We mentioned above that the group analyst and the analytic group are inserted into and become part of the unconscious organizational processes of the secure forensic setting, which can be considered from the perspective of the social defence/countertransference system (Jaques, 1955; Menzies, 1960; Robbins, 1993). The two clinical examples show group analysts wrestling to free themselves from their own inclinations to join in the large group's (hospital's) offer of sanctioned safety through projective identification and distance. This wider dynamic, as Main (1989) and Robbins (1993) point out, replicates at the system level many of the pathological aspects of patients' illnesses, and consequently reinforces the very psychopathology which is meant to be ameliorated. Our final example illustrates how a group of ward staff—eight nurses and one occupational therapist—meet with a group analyst to reflect on their work with patients and their interactions as a team, and how they must all contend with their inclination to ignore their participation in the large group (institutional) countertransference dynamics.

The proposed move to another building on the site is raised: "Is there any news about when this is going to happen?" The ward manager says that there is nothing definite yet, but it will probably be in about six months. There are further comments about having to go over to see the new place and the absence of a garden (there is a large one adjoining the present ward): "We'll only have a balcony there." A nurse who had previously worked in the other building said that there was a garden, but it was not easily reached: "Imagine, you need to go through thirteen doors from reception to the ward I used to work on!" There was joking, laughter and mock consternation from group members, with underlying anxieties about change, accessibility and boundaries.

The ward manager turns the conversation to a major review of forensic services and comments that he had expressed concern about the number of patients referred to the ward (a rehabilitation ward) who were clearly not rehab material. A senior nurse added his bewilderment: "How can we work with patients like X and Y? They've been around for years. And why has B suddenly been moved into the ward? He's too unwell." The ward manager clarifies that yes, it was, as they suspected, driven by the need for beds. "If we didn't take these patients, emergency admissions from prisons would be blocked, and anyway, where would the current unsuitable patients go? No other wards want them." "So they're just bed blockers," responded another nurse. "Yeah," joked another, "but take D, he's a famous bed blocker." There is considerable laughter and excitement.

Suddenly the mood shifts as the ward manger again refers to the service review. The problem is that the wards can have six, seven, eight consultant teams, none of which works in the same way. Doctors don't feel attached to the ward, are uncomfortable when they come, and rarely attend the weekly community meeting. Several group members mention that they think other wards have fewer consultant teams; but even if it could be simplified, the manager interjects, the admissions team would still have to hand over to the rehab team, and they might have different diagnoses. "Such problems could be overcome, but now the service is totally fragmented. It sounds exactly like the symptoms of schizophrenia," said the senior nurse.

The theme of hand-over prompts the Occupational Therapist (OT) to talk about the community meeting that morning, which of those present only she, one other nurse and the group analyst had attended. Did the manager know that a patient, Miss G, had said in the community meeting that he was a bully and should be removed, and that more white staff should be appointed? Miss G is black, and had expressed overt racist attitudes to the predominantly Asian and African staff. Yes, the manager had heard, and for some time he had tried to recruit a racially mixed team. The recent appointment panels had yielded four new staff. The OT commented further that in the community meeting after-group (for attending staff, and also conducted by the group analyst) people wondered why all the appointments were black and Asian. The manager proceeded to explain in an irritated tone, along with his rather defensive clinical team leader (CTL), that they had waited in vain for the two white applicants. "Not only did they not turn up," the CTL proclaimed contemptuously, "but they couldn't even show the consideration to phone!" They both went on to give some employment demographics to prove that while consultants, social workers and top managers are predominantly white, 85% of nursing trainees are non-white. "Whites don't want this work now, it's too low for them," said an Asian nursing assistant.

At this point the group analyst realized that a particular nurse who had attended the community meeting and the staff after-group, where he had been outspoken about the need to communicate today as a team, had not come to this group because he had "volunteered" for other duties so as to miss reflective practice. Another nurse present that morning was walking around the ward, visible to us all. Finally, the OT's only present colleague from the morning groups had maintained total silence. The group analyst decided to comment on the process of handing over, communicating, which the OT had broached without support from her silent, defecting and volunteering colleagues. He said that the schizophrenic system that had been recognized in relation to the consultant teams was believed to offer protection from something frightening which arose from contact and that this might be going on in front of us. Something was interfering with the hand-over right now, which made it easier to refer to a patient who had said that the manager was a bully, or to say that the consultant teams might have conflicting diagnoses of the patients.

The group analyst now approached the countertransference edge, for he was tempted to keep the thirteen secure doors closed, prevent any chance of being perceived as a destructive bully who moves the staff out of their psychic garden retreat (Steiner, 1993), and so evade contact with what he believed to be the crucial issue in this group: the silent nurse. For this nurse had, in the community meeting after-group (in the absence of the ward manager, the CTL, senior nurse and several others now present), spontaneously exploded when he was told that all the recently appointed staff were non-white (as he is) and that two were from the same ethnic group as the ward manager and most of the senior nursing staff: "He's done it again, he's appointed his own people!" Of course the preceding demographics lesson and explanation about the appointment panel had reinforced this nurse's defences, and with only the OT's indirect encouragement he felt unable to "hand over" his morning contribution. The group analyst pointed out the long-standing conviction in the staff group that Asian senior staff devalued their African subordinates; even the sole black senior nurse felt uncomfortable on a ward whose reputation as a fiefdom controlled by an "Asian mafia" had spread throughout the service. The silent member then plucked up the courage to say that he had entertained an image of a "bullying" manager who picked his own, and even allowed manipulation of the duty register so that "his" could work together. Some contact could then be made between a fantasy charged with belief and the external realities of recruitment, employment and promotion. It remains to be seen whether the persecutory dynamics projected into perceptions of race, which solidify division within this staff group, can be linked to the countertransference-driven dread which structures the staff-patient interactions and requires not security but thirteen *internal* doors.

Acknowledgement

We acknowledge the participation of Bob Harris and Adele Mason, who contributed to the supervision group held by the senior author (JG) in which some of the ideas in this chapter were developed.

CHAPTER FOUR

Bearable or unbearable? Unconscious communication in management

Michael Mercer

Introduction

Most examples in this book relate to the impact that forensic patients have on staff in direct clinical or treatment situations, but this chapter sets out to give an account of how the phenomenon of countertransference can be used to understand management dilemmas and to illuminate the difficulties faced by staff who are trying to work together in organisations to contain and treat forensic patients. The idea of countertransference is not an easy one to reconcile with the management task. The understanding of countertransference is largely based on clinical settings where action is restricted to talking and making interpretations. Management on the other hand is based on a wide range of actions, albeit hopefully thoughtful actions. The role of the manager is inseparable from action of some kind. Managers, even ones who began their careers as clinicians, do not on the whole spend much time thinking about their emotional responses to situations. The world of the manager generally precludes much detailed care for the relationships within organisations, and thinking is mostly considered a cognitive matter only.

An outcome is so often a requirement for managers that, at its worst, the means of achieving it can seem not to matter. Although one could say that action without thought would be a sign of not knowing what one is doing, managers are vulnerable to the view that doing nothing is not an option, or to the prejudice that thought is synonymous with inaction. First thoughts are considered better than second thoughts, because there is no time. Competence can be judged by speed.

The alternative view offered here is that emotional knowledge is an essential piece of the intelligence required by managers even if it takes time to investigate and understand. If managers do not know what other people are feeling and know what they themselves are feeling, vital information about the state of the organisation is lacking. Psychoanalysis persists in its view that thinking is an emotional matter. Thoughts require a mind. Thoughts are sentient. Emotions cause some thoughts to be overvalued or denied. Anxiety, guilt and pain lead to defences. Pleasure and excitement can be sought at the expense of reality. These human basics are expressed in and through relationships at work as anywhere else. Human relationships are ubiquitous, and groups are emotional places. Work is carried out by people who have relationships with their work, and this is especially true when people are also the subject of the work, as in the mental health field.

The manager and the institution

The central part of this chapter is an account of a management problem in a forensic mental health service. The description of the way this problem is presented to a management workshop tries to highlight different ways in which countertransference can be expressed and how countertransference can affect thinking. As a consequence of experiencing the impact of the work and the form of its presentation to the workshop, it was possible to achieve a very different view of the problem to the one which was first presented. It modified considerably the manager's view of his task. Whilst in some respects it was somewhat depressing in its conclusions, the overall achievement of this work was to enable the manager to find a new direction and appreciation of the depth of the management task. These are outcomes which are extremely undervalued in a climate of target-driven activity. The means by which this was done was a particular kind of listening to responses in myself as the consultant and in the group of colleagues in the workshop. The kind of listening described is an attempt to formulate for the task of management what in psychoanalysis would be called "working with the countertransference".

In the workshop, a multidisciplinary group of managers, mainly managers of professional clinical staff, present and discuss with colleagues issues of current concern. The topics presented have ranged widely. They include such matters as staff supervision, the management of teams, multidisciplinary working, professional identity, and the development of policy. The overall task of the group has been the study of the role of the clinical manager in the institution.

Repeated themes include the psychological weaknesses of a small but significant number of staff who are liable to take long term sick leave, the problems of recruiting sufficiently high calibre staff, the false accusations and complaints made by patients against staff, the management of aggressive and disturbed patients, the interface with legal agencies, the interracial mixes of staff and patients, and the rapid development of services for special groups of patients. There is a context of constantly trying to maintain a secure physical environment for both staff and patients. Whilst many of these difficulties are shared with other public mental health services, the severity of the mental disturbance and the constant risk of violence are very evident.

For the most part these challenges are met with hard work, integrity and a high level of skill and experience. However, this work is also confusing, frightening and frustrating. Anxiety levels are high. Panic attacks amongst staff are quite common. Staff, particularly nursing staff, are assaulted, occasionally seriously. It is worth emphasising that the forensic patients for whom the service is responsible have often been violent, sometimes to the extent of homicide. These patients can be either very remote and out of contact with themselves and with staff or intensely intrusive and provocative in their relationships. Whilst disturbed and disturbing behaviours are not always everyday occurrences, they are an everyday presence. The underlying mental condition of this group of patients is almost always going to be chronic and will be very difficult to treat. Their capacity to develop meaningful lives will be restricted even in the best outcomes.

These limitations present considerable challenges to clinical teams and their morale. The capacity to remain thoughtful in the face of such damage, whether caused by physical or psychic violence, is finite, and such capacity has to be developed over time through the assimilation of experience. This is as true for managers as it is for clinicians. The current political and policy concerns about the treatment and containment of those who commit acts of violence whilst mentally ill overlook too easily the issues of how much change it is possible to effect. Whilst some major changes (such as the declining role of Special Hospitals, increased facilities for women or proposed legislation that is likely to make it easier to detain individuals with a propensity to violence) may be desirable on humanitarian or clinical grounds, the fact remains that very few of these patients will show significant changes in psychopathology. The emotional burden for both staff and managers trying to improve matters can only be increased by public expectation of magical solutions. Keeping mentally alive and alert in this situation is very difficult.

This is not just a matter of external reality. The implications of the kind of thinking represented in this book are to be taken seriously. When the necessary psychological capacity is so lacking in these patients, the hopelessness and guilt they would have to face in order to develop psychically is projected into the staff, but also into the services. Whilst the inevitable tensions between containment and rehabilitation remain an important matter, the problems for the service in managing projected hopelessness and guilt are underestimated. Although the current pace of change is hectic, the inherent limit in the capacity of human systems to bear hopelessness is constantly ignored. Recent concerns about the treatment of violent adolescents and the treatment of disturbed offenders in prisons bear a sad testimony to this fact.

The primary task of managers includes providing a setting in which clinicians can continue to remain in contact with their patients. There is a physical setting to this task to which the staff become surprisingly accustomed: locked wards, monitored entry systems, alarms, secure places to interview patients, and so forth. There is also a procedural setting requiring security checks of one kind and another, drug tests, searches, observational procedures, investigations, etc. Management in the broad sense of the term is responsible for ensuring that both patients and staff interact in a safe environment. However, there is also a setting based on the relationships between staff members of which it is vital to be aware. Staff have to rely on each other. Is this reliance trustworthy and in good order? Do people do what they say they are going to do? Are there responsive and responsible relations between senior and junior staff, between the different disciplines, between managers and clinicians? What is the balance between critical attitudes and sympathetic support? This need for relational security also includes the patients. It has always been the first criterion of staff security that they need to know their patients. Knowing the states of mind of patients, knowing what provokes them, knowing significant events that are occurring, all profoundly influence the capacity of the staff to create a safe environment.

The setting in this relational sense is often infused with psychic violence and its consequences. For example, in one workshop presentation in which the manager was preoccupied with the dynamics of his team and his involvement with them, phrases such as "stormy" were used. The threats to leave by one of the team members were described as having "the impact of an assault". One workshop participant on another occasion described herself as "steaming" after a meeting. A colleague was described as "rude, angry, easily stressed and condescending", and when confronted, the colleague was described as "fragile". Another group of staff were described as "a vicious bunch". Taken individually, these phrases are not in themselves particularly remarkable, but when listened to with a sensitive ear, they create a picture in which it becomes clear that however amiable overt relationships might be, staff relationships in forensic settings frequently acquire a violent tone. This tone is not always explicit and conscious, and staff are not always aware of its impact. It usually becomes normalised as part of day-to-day experience. Indeed, in normal circumstances it would be seen as a necessary release that such feelings can be expressed without too much anxiety, provided good normal working relationships are maintained. However, it can also be seen in relationships between the disciplines in management meetings which are not productive, for instance where there are conflicts about chairing meetings and the way business is conducted, or where there are unexpected withdrawals from meetings, or where miscommunications occur about the implementation of a care plan. This book contains many examples of this sort of experience in which relationships, and thus the setting for the work, become infused with aggressive attitudes and behaviours.

The specific process by which this takes place is known to psychoanalysis as projective identification, and it is part of the phenomenon of countertransference. A split takes place in the self when there is too much anxiety or pain. The self then places the unbearable experience, be it of pain or anxiety or guilt, in an object. This object might be an actual external object or an object internal to the mind. A projection takes place of the disowned part, which is then identified with the object. In the forensic setting, the violent and ill parts of the patients, and also the healthier but frightened and intimidated parts of the personality, become located in the setting, especially the clinical staff who have responsibility for their care. In her original description of the concept, Melanie Klein (1946) made clear that this is an unconscious process. In the example of the use of violent language about colleagues, the staff concerned were not aware at the time of the extent to which they were giving voice to aggressive thoughts. It is only with distance and hindsight that it becomes clear that they are being affected by unconscious processes.

Since the concept was first formulated by Klein over fifty years ago, there has been much development of its implications as a fundamental form of human communication. Distinctions are made, for instance, between projective identification in both normal and pathological forms of communication. In the normal version of projective identification, when we feel understood, we can claim back the temporarily projected part and feel a more whole person as a result of the mutual communication. It is the means by which we have a sense of understanding the other person and being understood. But projective identification can also take a more pathological form when parts of the personality are disowned. This is the form that is alluded to above when violent language is used. The forcefulness of the projection is intended to rid the self permanently of the unbearable experience and the part of mind that can know about such an experience. The receiving object then becomes unconsciously contaminated. It is common for the object to experience this as a more uncomfortable state of mind.

However, although this process is well understood in clinical settings, it remains difficult to make good use of it more widely within organisations. This is in part because psychoanalysis is not the most common source of theory in mental health or in management, even though no other theoretical formulation as yet does justice to the phenomena, but it is also because the processes referred to are unconscious, and it requires a certain setting and capacity to become aware of them. It is also an obvious fact of life that pain and anxiety are inevitable and human beings develop defences against them. The capacity to bear such knowledge and feeling is limited. This is nowhere more starkly clear than in forensic services. When in disturbed states of minds, the patients have committed horrendous acts. Human beings often do terrible things to each other in the ordinary social and political world, but these patients also suffer from severely disturbed states of mind, and frequently have very disturbed and disturbing personal histories. Any contact between patient and setting therefore has to take into account how much the patient can know about themselves and how much knowledge the staff can tolerate.

Workshop setting

In order to take account of these processes and the way they affect the work, it is necessary to create a setting to study them, similar in many respects to the clinical one. A workshop was established, with myself as consultant, for clinical managers to discuss their work. Over time these workshops have developed a spontaneity and security which have allowed much useful learning. Although the members of the workshop may have some contact with each other in the course of their work, the setting has an authority of its own apart from the organisation, and this helps to create a freer atmosphere. Although my role as consultant has its own authority, a significant part of the structure of the workshop is that all its members have equal authority. Each member participates, taking responsibility for the confidentiality of the workshop, for the way they bring their knowledge of the organisation, and for being committed to the task of learning and development. Outside of the workshop, in their ordinary organisational roles, their authority relationships will vary. No actions are decided on in the workshop.

It exists solely to promote thinking, and the members remain responsible for their work and their relationships with colleagues. At the same time it is an important opportunity to understand and learn from each other, which contributes much towards improving relations between the disciplines.

Whilst being based in one kind of objective reality, in which observation, theory, analysis and problem-solving are important, the workshop also allows for freedom in selection of topic, manner of presentation and emotional communication, which creates a sentient picture of the presenter's relationship with their work. There is also an awareness that a significant relationship exists within the workshop between the presenter and the group. Listening in this way develops an attitude of mind, similar to the psychoanalyst, in which receptiveness to the unanticipated and subtle emergence of significant actions and affects is developed. What is absent is as important potentially as what is present, and significant diagnostic signs are over-determined. The same problem is likely to appear in several different ways at different levels.

As time goes by, work discussion groups of this type allow for a limited degree of personal disclosure about the responses of the presenter to the problems in hand, and facilitate an approach of learning from experience. This question of what personal disclosure is appropriate is an important one, particularly because it takes place in the context of ongoing relationships with colleagues. I think it should be assumed that personal disclosure in the sense of personal history or private fantasy should not be encouraged. This would be a serious confusion. However, the emotional freedom with which people can speak of their work and their emotional responses to it is very important. There are sometimes occasions when a presenter feels overwhelmed. I think it is very important at these moments for the consultant to be properly aware of the vulnerability of the presenter, and the most helpful response is to continue in a sensitive way whilst acknowledging the impact of the work. An instance occurs in the example which follows.

Being able to study the relationship of the presenter to their work in this way allows for the clarification of the processes involved, sometimes enabling implicit beliefs to become conscious and so potentially available to change. The assumption is that the better the view of reality, a reality which includes emotions and motivations, the better the quality of thinking. An important effect of this setting and its approach is that there can be a readjustment to the balance of what the presenting manager is and is not responsible for. It is this readjustment which is the basis of development and can potentially lead to improvements in job satisfaction and performance. An example of a presentation from the workshop, disguised for reasons of confidentiality, illustrates a number of issues from the point of view of both the management task and the value of understanding countertransference.

Case study

Mr A, an experienced manager of day activity services, began his presentation to the group by saying that he wanted to bring a problem between two members of staff. Together they were providing a newly commissioned day activity service, based in a separate and special Unit within the Trust, for which he had only recently assumed responsibility. One of these staff, well established in the Unit, he had not known previously, and the other staff member, new to this Unit, was known to him from her work elsewhere. The more established worker had been given clinical lead status for the day service. The new worker had been appointed recently by the Head of Department who had commissioned this new day service. This Head of Department had then left the Trust, leaving Mr A, one of her deputies, to run the service.

The initial presentation to the workshop was of a problem about supervision and in the relations between the two staff. Mr A's emphasis was rather definite, as though the workshop were in some way expected to concur unquestioningly with his view, although I thought that the tone he used was uncharacteristically dogmatic for Mr A, who is normally more flexible in the way he presents. This general tone also alerted the members of the workshop to the language which was being used to describe the situation. Mr A implied that he respected the newly appointed worker, but he described the established worker as "inherited", which conveyed a sense of her not being wanted. Mr A had also not been involved in the appointment of the new worker, which had been made by the Head of Department before leaving. This contributed to the impression that Mr A did not feel properly and equally responsible for these two staff. I thought it was also noteworthy that initially the context of the Unit in which these staff worked seemed to be missing or even dismissed as unimportant. This contributed to a sense that Mr A's taking over responsibility for this new service was hasty and not thought through. The workshop had not yet been told what this Unit was or why the responsibility for this work had been transferred to Mr A. The problem was presented as being one of staff management and supervision.

This initial omission was corrected as Mr A went on to explain that this new day activity service was in a special Unit for a disturbed patient group who had presented particular risks of aggression to staff and also of self-harm and sometimes suicide. The staff responsible for the day-to-day care of these patients had previously adopted an approach which used a significant level of individual seclusion and intensive observation on the grounds that the patients were not safe to interact with each other. The development of the new service for which Mr A was now responsible was intended to improve the level of therapeutic care through the development of day activities and by allowing the patients more interaction.

The new service had multidisciplinary agreement from the managers concerned and additional management time had been approved. However, this extra commitment by the other disciplines had not been forthcoming, and Mr A was apparently left with sole management responsibility. The sense of disinterest in the Unit for this new day service was manifested in a powerful way when the new service was found to have been allocated space in a corridor, but without any circulation or activity space for the patient activity which had been agreed. Listening to this account, it was striking that so little resentment was expressed by Mr A about this withdrawal of support and resources. It was interesting that when discussion started, the workshop members felt resentful on his behalf at his being left with such a mess.

Mr A continued his presentation, saying that when he took up his new role and visited the Unit, he found that the new member of staff was very upset and disappointed and in considerable conflict with her more established colleague. In Mr A's presentation this was spoken of as though the rest had been background and this was coming to the real problem that he wished to present. However, the content of the conflict between the colleagues was not referred to directly; rather, it was implied that it was of a sensitive nature and particularly difficult. Mr A instead made references to the lack of staff appraisals, and he felt that carrying them out would be a help. In a rather throwaway manner he commented that the new worker was going to prepare a report which would probably "slag off" the new service. Although this was presented as though the workshop were being presented with the heart of the matter, in fact the workshop members looked anxious and confused, a response I also shared.

Mr A continued to assert that this was a supervision problem, and he had begun by seeing the two staff members individually. This for some reason had put him in an awkward position. I speculated to myself that perhaps this was because the staff had spoken to him about each other in a very hostile way. He decided to try a new approach and had started to see them together. These discussions had led to difficulties and had raised questions about confidentiality and how secure the workers felt. Mr A was going to try and resolve this by adopting a business meeting style of supervision. However, he was unhappy about doing this and felt it was something of a failure. He made a reference to this issue having raised personal issues for himself. At this point he finished his presentation and seemed to hand the problem over to the group, as though he felt helpless.

What of the countertransference so far? This particular presentation elicited a range of responses in the workshop and in myself as consultant. The impact of the presentation was to make the workshop quite anxious without being able to determine what was the most important issue to think about. Clearly difficult matters were being raised about the relationship between the staff, but the content of this was rather confused and inexplicit. The references to confidentiality imposed a constraint on how far it was appropriate to explore them. This experience of constraint was further highlighted by the unusually restrictive way in which the circumstances of this Unit emerged. The way in which Mr A brought in personal references at the end and his defensiveness about his work also created a feeling of having to be careful, perhaps to the extent that developing the discussion in the usual open way would be felt by Mr A as persecuting and critical.

There was a sense of discontinuity which was most striking. Mr A and his work were well known to the group and generally had a sensitivity and thoughtfulness, but on this occasion there was a strongly dogmatic tone which alerted everyone to an uncharacteristic defensiveness in Mr A. We all felt that we had to be careful in what we said in order to protect Mr A. I think it was clear to the group that something quite serious was going wrong. It was very unusual for Mr A to personalise difficulties by focusing on individual staff almost to the exclusion of understanding the organisational context. This uncharacteristic certainty on Mr A's part seemed to suggest that a more sensitive capacity in him had been suppressed, perhaps rather violently. The sense of hopelessness and anxiety observable in Mr A by the workshop was in fact being experienced by the group, whilst Mr A appeared to be in a position of certainty about the approach he had adopted.

The ways in which countertransference is elicited are complex and many. Most analysts would agree that it is possible for the analyst to experience a direct transfer of unconscious feeling from the patient that need not be communicated through words. Subtle qualities of tone and manner are often sufficient. At the same time these communications are not easy to interpret. In a workshop where members of the group know each other quite well, one of the important forms of communication is the discontinuity, the way in which the presentation is uncharacteristic of the person. It may be that the specific issue being presented reveals a limitation of a personal kind, but it will always be linked to sensitivity to some form of projection. I think in this example it is possible to infer that Mr A is being influenced by an emotional tone surrounding the new service which is restricting his capacity to think and to manage, and it will be important to address the forcefulness with which this is happening. This experience caused a noteworthy level of anxiety in the workshop.

Through slowly opening up discussion in the workshop of Mr A's experience and the responsibility he had been given, other aspects of the situation came to light. The Unit was characterised by a paranoid atmosphere in which it was not considered possible to help these patients. Seclusion was the preferred response to any sign of violence or aggression by a patient. Managers did not generally visit the Unit. Mr A felt anxious that if he took up the issues raised by his staff about the Unit, then the managers of the other staff would react adversely and become more restrictive. The atmosphere in the Unit was that it was too risky to "tread on toes", and Mr A felt anxious about discussing the problems of the Unit in a wider organisational way. At the same time, in the discussion, Mr A became more defensive of himself and wished also to protect his staff, as though he felt that what he had said might sound critical of them. Having begun his presentation in an energetic and businesslike way, he now became less certain and was obviously affected in some emotional way. Uncharacteristically, he again indicated that some idiosyncratic aspects of the situation reminded him of personal matters.

It is necessary to be thoughtful about why Mr A is so affected by this situation and to consider the seriousness of this impact before the possible roles and responsibilities can be clarified. In listening to this countertransference response, it became possible to see that very similar experiences were being described by Mr A himself in relation to the Unit. He had felt shut out and let down by his fellow managers and the atmosphere of the Unit just as the workshop had felt shut out by the lack of openness in his presentation. What he had described as feeling "risky" was being replicated in the workshop, where there was defensiveness and anxiety. The new service had not been given the physical space to develop, and neither was the workshop given the psychic space to develop its work. The sense of seclusion, as the only response to very disturbing and aggressive behaviour which was characteristic of the Unit, was brought into the workshop in the form of Mr A's unusual isolation from his colleagues and his restrictions in thinking about his role.

Through voicing these kinds of observations in the workshop it became possible to look at some important aspects of the way in which the total organisational state of the Unit was reflected in the interpersonal experience of the staff concerned. The tensions that had arisen between the new worker and the established worker were also an expression of the way in which the Unit reacted to a new service being established. The new worker, keen to try new activities and "open things up", was met with opposition from the more established one. This took the form of her being made to feel that she did not understand the severity of the patients' disturbance and how necessary it was to adopt a more security-conscious approach.

Mr A significantly identified with the new worker and this conflict between old and new. Mr A had just the same experience with his own management colleagues, who did not appear to take his arrival seriously. He felt less sympathetic towards the established worker, with whom he found it difficult to communicate.

His mixed and ambivalent feelings led to his adopting a "businesslike" approach to supervision and to attempt joint meetings, to bring them together. This is an interesting response: practical in an obvious way, but also diagnostic of the difficulty. It was failing because the "businesslike" approach excluded the necessary sentient communication about what was taking place. However, at the same time it expressed a proper wish to bring the old Unit and the new service together. The fact that it was being undertaken in this particular way, in which the context of the Unit was being excluded, was significant. It was clear that the anxiety experienced within the workshop was indicative of serious anxiety in the Unit itself about its functioning and the problems it faced with its disturbed patients. A "blind eye" was being turned to the extreme seriousness of the problems of aggression, self-harm and suicide. The development of a proposed day activity programme was ineffective, yet at the same time acted as a diversion. This "solution" located the despair facing the whole Unit in the new worker and the new service. It was rather shocking for the workshop to learn a few weeks later that this new worker had resigned.

As these experiences began to emerge in the workshop discussion, Mr A became upset and shocked. He realised the extent of the management difficulties facing him in developing the new service as the significance of the relationship between the new service and the Unit became clear. He and the workshop became quite depressed at the seriousness of it, but at the same time they also began to recover some realistic sense of the management task. It looked as though this new service had not been set up to solve a problem, but rather there was an implicit expectation that it would fail, allowing the status quo to be reaffirmed. At first it was not at all clear what could be achieved, but it was important that Mr A's proper but limited responsibility could be recovered. He was able to rebalance his view of his role and relinquish the unconscious burden of having to rescue a whole Unit in serious difficulty. He could also recover from being entrapped in personal staff relationships which had become the home for institutional anxiety and conflict. This new balance allowed him to think more freely about how to support his staff.

It was also important to realise that there were important management responsibilities being neglected. By only working on the supervisory relationships, Mr A had avoided the more difficult task of taking up with the other managers in the Unit the real purpose of the new service and the way in which they had undermined its being established. This work would take time, cause anxiety and discomfort, and involve a much wider discussion than had taken place so far. From an initial position of thinking that there was only a limited management role in relation to the staff, the realisation that there was a much greater management task was quite depressing.

A work discussion group such as this, which allows both the content of the work and the manner of its presentation to be studied, is able to draw attention to essential aspects of the management task. In the day-to-day work managers are used to problem-solving, keeping things moving and thinking about the specifics of what is required. In the longer term there is policy formulation, planning future changes, responding to external requirements that are imposed, and so forth. This kind of work discussion draws attention to the network of relationships in which complex policy decisions are made, and highlights the fluctuating balance within it between the capacity for defensive anti-task behaviour and the potential for resourcefulness in support of the task. Relationships are both the means by which work in organisations is carried out and the means by which a painful task is avoided. Very often what is revealed, as in this instance, is that these relationships require more work and care, and that many of these other management functions are a displacement activity to avoid facing painful issues.

Discussion

Relationships within organisations have three different dimensions, all of which can be seen in the example above. There is a dimension which is institutional, a dimension based on roles and a personal dimension. These three levels, institution, role and personal come together in the experience of working in the organisation, and they are all interrelated. A manager needs to have all three in mind and to be able to move between them flexibly, or problems and stress are generated.

At the level of the institution, the Unit presented to the workshop is having serious difficulties in its work of caring for this group of disturbed, self-harming patients. The response of shutting these aggressive patients away and taking up a distant observing, custodial function is defensive. It allows the institution to guard against fear and a feeling of failure. The response of attempting to develop a day activity programme has the appearance of a more helpful attitude, but it is set up in such a way that it is bound to fail. The managers and staff with the primary responsibility for the Unit made it clear by their behaviour that they could not face becoming more involved with their patients, and they split off this responsibility to a new service which could not by itself bring about change. This was a defensive response to severe depressive and paranoid anxieties. It only succeeded in splitting off despair and failure by locating it in a newly created team with its new manager. No serious attempt was apparently made to integrate the management of the day service with the general management of the Unit. With the resignation of the new staff member, the failure of the new enterprise to change anything is apparent and the defensive view of the task is maintained. There appears to be an absence of management at the institutional level.

At the personal level, Mr A has substantial experience and ability, which he has proved in other contexts by being asked to take on more senior positions. Indeed, this particular example arose partly because he was thought of as a clinical manager who could do the job of developing a service in a difficult situation. He has energy for the work and took up the role positively. He engaged actively with the problems that were presented to him by the staff, and he tried flexibly to find a solution. He also had the intuition to know that there was discrepancy between the way he was approaching this particular project and his normal approach. Whilst not initially being able to identify what this discrepancy was, he felt there was a problem with which he needed help and which he needed to bring to the group. The quality of Mr A's intuition is also evidenced by his response to the problem of trying to bring the two staff members together. Whilst not a solution to the problem, it did indicate that Mr A has an emotional valency to try to work to bring things together.

There was also some reason why this particular problem caused an intrusion into his personal life, which he expressed in a general way at the end of his presentation. It is important that the question of what the personal matter might be is not explored, but rather that it is used to indicate the degree of intrusion that is felt in the work situation and the consequent strength of the defences that are in place institutionally. In general, and in this particular instance, it is most likely to indicate guilt of some kind. This can be understood by the consultant to help diagnose the emotional significance of the presented material. However, it is also important that a group or a consultant or a senior manager is able to recognise that the work is taking a personal toll on their staff.

Although the issue does not arise in this particular example, the personal valencies of staff and their suitability for this work is a further matter. The workshop repeatedly raises instances of the problems of staff who are on long-term sick leave, who may have suffered seriously from assaults by patients and who are not recovering. Conflicts surrounding personnel matters such as grading are also frequently a diversion from a lack of emotional capacity to sustain the work with these patients. Managing these matters is very time-consuming and draining.

Whilst both these aspects, institutional and personal, come into the work discussion, the main focus of the workshop is on exploring the third dimension, the role of the clinical manager. Taking up the role is the primary responsibility, and whilst the institutional level and the personal level need to be understood, how the work is carried out is the central matter. The rebalancing of the elements in the role is the most important factor in helping managers develop and become more effective.

Mr A's initial focus was on the supervisory function. In this area he felt competent and could use his capacities. This was in contrast to what could be seen in the Unit as a whole, which was that the new service would not solve the inherent difficulties. Yet Mr A felt responsible for them. The greatest difficulty was in taking up those aspects of the role which involved trying to ensure that the service had the opportunity to develop. It did not have the necessary facilities. The requisite management meetings were not in place. There was no adequate referral system, and so on. All of these aspects of the role would require work, contact with the hostile attitude of other staff, and perhaps contact with a real sense of failure and frustration. This rebalancing of his role which could take place after the working through in the group was a real help to him.

In a forensic setting, this necessary integration of institution, role and the personal comes under particular pressures. The example in the presentation is of a Unit which is functioning in a particularly poor and defensive manner, and inevitably paranoid anxieties infect the work at each of the three levels. The fears concerning failure, the preoccupation with security, a tendency to behave in a dogmatic way, constant anxieties about confronting individuals, and the intrusive levels of personal stress that are suffered by the staff, evidenced in this account, are all endemic to this work. The necessary integration of institution, role and the individual allows for a complex system of projections of the particularly unbearable aspects of the work.

This account of the way both paranoid and depressive anxieties invade the capacity to work and think, through projective processes, also requires a consideration of the superego. This was the first internal object recognised by Freud, the part of the mind which is set over and against the ego, socially manifested as a conscience and an ego ideal. From the outset, Freud viewed the superego as a primary source of difficulty which prevents the normal processes of life through an excessively harsh attitude, using guilt to persecute and control the ego, which is trying to balance internal and external needs. Recently, psychoanalysts have renewed theoretical interest in the differences between a more benign version of the superego which supports the ego in its task of facing up to reality and a pathological persecutory superego which sets out to rule and punish.

Forensic patients, contrary to popular belief, do not on the whole suffer from a lack of superego, but rather from an excess of the persecutory kind of superego, which is so unbearable that it is projected externally. Facing the court, for example, is less frightening than having nightmares. There are of course other cases, generally known as psychopathic, where the absence of a superego, or the presence of a highly distorted and projected one, is a part of the clinical picture. But here similarly the fate of normal superego development is of particular interest. In psychotic individuals the superego takes on a particularly terrifying quality. The role of the superego is also a primary feature of management in such a setting, and should be considered within the overall perspective of learning from countertransference and projected states.

Firstly, consider the functioning of the superego in the institution. Most policy changes would fall under this category. There is an obvious conflict of interest, for example, between the need for public protection and the taking of reasonable clinical risks in the release of patients. Yet it is quite possible for policy decisions to go in each of these directions at the same time without facing the difficulty of making these decisions. It is easy to be "right" in a kind of righteous way, as a manager or a politician to lead in one direction whilst being able to ignore the constraints of the other. This kind of context for instance makes it extremely difficult in many cases for clinical teams to make balanced recommendations to tribunals.

When the management of risk becomes a superego activity, it operates as though risk can be eliminated, for example by following a particular procedure. In effect this achieves a relinquishing of responsibility for difficult and anxious situations by a state of mind of denial and detachment. Living with the inevitable anxieties regarding risk assessment is replaced by a transitory conviction that one is protected simply by having done the "right" thing. This disownment leads to a projection of the unbearable into a part of the organisation which is not empowered for the task. It is clear that the development of the new day activity service was a response of this kind. It appeared to deal with the guilt experienced by the Unit and its managers that a proper treatment and humane environment were not being provided. The development was, however, not thought through and integrated with the Unit and its primary problems. Projection of total responsibility into the day service ensured that the staff there felt a failure and felt guilty.

The individual manager in the presented example had a superego which functioned in both a benign and a pathological way, often in response to projections. The way the manager initially fitted in with being given responsibility for this service would in some instances be helpful. As a manager it can help to have a tolerance of frustration which helps one get on with the job, when so much is going to be less than perfect. However, fitting in and being helpful can become a blindness and a compliance based on a fear of aggressiveness. Perhaps in this example it would have been more helpful to ask more questions before accepting responsibility for such a difficult task.

There is a superego element involved in tackling the staff relations issue by doing things right, thinking about appraisals and being businesslike. Being identified with a superego position in this way protects the manager against the feeling of being confused and not knowing what to do. At the same time there is a helpful element at work which allows Mr A to bring his difficulties to the right place, the workshop, where he can be helped to think and relinquish the superego response, which is too limited.

I think in this instance, and many others, it is possible to see the severity of the superego which occurs in forensic institutions and the way in which the extremely distorted and pathological superego of the patients becomes split off and projected into staff and parts of the organisation. The combination of madness alongside badness leaves little room for ameliorating their severity. It is possible with ordinary delinquent badness to perceive the element of madness in it, and this increases the capacity for sympathy and the wish to help in a reforming way. Similarly with madness, it is possible to tolerate the badness of it, by understanding that the individual has limited responsibility for their state of mind. However, when badness and madness occur together, this leaves little room for reparation. There is too much to do, too little healthy mind to work with, and the only response to it can be to lock it away as unacceptable and unbearable.

Conclusion

This chapter has attempted to describe some of the complex ways in which an organisation such as a forensic mental health service operates, as seen through the psychoanalytic perspective of countertransference. This concept potentially allows managers to think more deeply about their roles and achieve a better balance between the three levels of institution, role and personal. It can help distinguish between defensive actions and the more meaningful and substantive engagement with the relationships within human institutions.

The chapter describes a particular kind of learning which requires a special setting in order to develop, usually in the form of consultation or workshop. This is a place where the ordinary authority relationships can to some degree be suspended in favour of authority based on enquiry and experience, which allows the relationship of a manager to their work to be observed and elaborated. Then the different sentient experiences, the discrepancies and repetitions, omissions, enactments and countertransference experiences can be given meaning. Such a setting relaxes some of the more common superego responses which foreclose consideration of human responses in organisations, and creates space for more healthy and realistic investigation.

Whilst it is true that this sort of attention is only possible to learn in a detailed way in a special setting, in practice the approach is supportive of management in an ordinary sense. The dichotomy offered at the beginning of the chapter between action and thought is obviously a false one. But detailed listening to emotional responses in the way that this workshop achieves underlines the great importance of the ordinary attention to emotional life within a management role. The simple lesson to be learnt from the study of the superego is to not be too ready to take up a critical attitude towards the apparent mistakes or emotional problems of staff or colleagues. Closer attention is likely to reveal that there is an indication of a problem of an organisational kind. Managers should expect staff to be affected by the emotional climate, and indeed should be concerned if they are not, because institutional defences will be developing. Managers should be attentive to their own intuition, especially when they sense that something might be going wrong. Intuitions are more likely to be right than not. Managers should notice both repetitions and idiosyncrasies in their staff. Anything out of the ordinary is worth paying closer attention to. Spending time talking and listening to staff is very important. Managers should be ready to talk through issues and seek to be less dominated by fears of failure.

These are all ordinary examples of being thoughtfully human in working with people, but the concept of countertransference makes the important link between emotion and task. Attention to colleagues and staff is part of the work if there is appreciation of the difficulty of the work and the knowledge that we are all faced with experiences we cannot bear.

CHAPTER FIVE

Thoughts from consulting in secure settings: do forensic institutions need psychotherapy?

Stanley Ruszczynski

> 4.2.26. Three matters concerned the team . . . The focus of clinical discussion and decision-making was predominantly on social behaviour and administrative and risk issues, rather than on seeking a psychological understanding of the patient . . . Whilst the assessment was good, there were shortcomings in the application of those assessments to help understand the offending behaviour and to design an appropriate treatment programme: ". . . What is needed is a clear and shared understanding of the patients' psychopathology, the reasons for their offending, psychologically, and to keep those in mind as targets of treatment and to monitor how treatment progresses."
>
> 4.2.28. Second, arrangements for the clinical supervision of ward-based staff did not appear to be sufficiently systematic and well organised. Such supervision is particularly important in the context of work with personality disordered patients.
>
> 4.2 29. Third, the Unit lacked highly experienced psychodynamic contributions to the assessment and treatment of its patients. This would complement the other approaches to

assessment and would help a vigilant awareness of the depth of the patients' psychopathology.

> 4.4.23. Dr O . . . gave evidence . . . on behalf of the Royal Collage of Psychiatrists . . . He invited us to pay regard to what he regarded as the "toxic emotional processes" in Special Hospitals: "We are dealing with the most disturbed individuals in society, incarcerated with each other for a very long period of time, working with staff groups who are also there for a very long period of time, and there is a corrosive effect on the staff group unless in fact management is aware of this, unless all the staff groups are in touch with this." [Ashworth Special Hospital: Report of the Committee of Inquiry, Vol. 1, January 1999, pp. 318, 324]

These quotes from the Fallon Report could be read as offering a criticism of the functioning of Ashworth Hospital in the mid-1990s. There is little doubt that it was warranted at that time. Institutions which have the remit for working with the most difficult mental health patients in our society will inevitably struggle in their duty of care, and they will arouse the concern of fellow professionals, politicians and the public. All high- and medium-secure hospital and prison settings will, from time to time, raise this concern. However, to read the comments simply as criticisms is a mistake. What these comments also point to is, I believe, a development in the ways forensic and personality disorder services need to be thought about. This development is the product of our growing understanding of the nature of these patients and the type of care, containment and treatment they require (Hinshelwood, 2001; Newrith, Meux & Taylor, 2006).

The Fallon report is wide-ranging, but the quotes given above represent a discernible approach in the document which regularly refers to shared understandings, clinical supervision of ward-based staff, different contributions complementing each other, toxic processes in special hospitals, the patient group, the staff group and management. In other words, what are being addressed, not surprisingly, are the various relationships and systems which make up the *institution* within which the patients are offered and staff attempt to provide containment and treatment. The significance of this perspective is my starting point.

In this chapter I will focus on those patients who are contained in institutions such as prisons and medium- and high-secure hospitals. I take it as given that some of the patients whom we encounter in the forensic and personality disorder services, whose disturbance and dangerousness as expressed through their criminal, perverse or violent actions are a central factor, may have the potential to benefit from one or more of a variety of individual and/or group therapeutic interventions, be that as inpatients or in the community. However, I will argue that for such patients the institution as a whole offers the most significant possibility for treatment and is in essence the primary therapeutic agent.

Hence I take the question in my title literally and answer it in the affirmative. I outline a view that, quite appropriately and necessarily, the institution itself, the institution as a group of clinical staff and of supporting administrative, security and management staff, all with the shared task of containing and managing the patients, benefits from the opportunity to reflect on, think about and try to understand the nature of its work with its patients. I base my thinking on my experience of consulting to a wide range of forensic institutions. I am not denying, of course, that the patients' states of mind and behaviours also need careful and considered attention (Cartwright, 2002; Morgan & Ruszczynski, 2007; Perelberg, 1999).

The therapeutic function I want to discuss is informed by psychoanalytic principles. Central to this is the capacity to observe, think about and try to understand the multiple dynamic interactions between the patients, between the staff, and between the staff and patients. Referring to interactions I am thinking not only of behaviour but also of attitudes, perspectives and emotional states. Further, there is the crucial issue of how this understanding is communicated to the patients so that they might assimilate not only some understanding of the ways in which they function, but also some of this capacity to try to reflect and think about emotions, impulses and experiences rather than act them out. And further, there is the question of how this is done alongside the necessity for the physical security of the staff and the physical containment of these dangerous patients (Parker, 2007; Pfäfflin & Adshead, 2004).

This stance, of course, is the clinical stance taken by the practitioner informed by psychoanalytic principles, and one within which the dynamics of the transference-countertransference relationship is central. It is taken as read that the nature of the relationship between the patient and the clinician will be informed by the patient's internal object relationships—his or her patterns of expectations, assumptions, fears and hopes born out of life experiences (actual and emotional). This will be parallelled by the nature of the patient's relationship to multiple others, to groups and to the institution as a whole. Who and what is the other (be that individual, group or institution) in the patient's conscious and unconscious mind? Striving to address this question requires careful attention to the details of the ways in which patients and staff interact with each other at a conscious and an unconscious level. The clinician's affective response and reaction to the patient—the countertransference—becomes a rich source of understanding of the patient when it is considered alongside knowledge of the patient's history, the nature of their offending behaviour and the ways in which they relate to those around them.

A central clinical and management fact about forensic patients, as with psychotic and borderline patients, is that they act upon their environment—both physically, whereby they can be hostile, aggressive, violent, unreachable, seductive, sexually perverse or violent, and also psychically, whereby they can generate states of mind in those around them which are disturbing and militate against reflection and thought. Difficult patients are difficult because they generate difficult feelings in us (Hinshelwood, 1999).

Forensic patients, by definition, also invade, corrupt, attack and damage the institutions which hold them. This is not said as a criticism but as a description of the psychological functioning of the patients we are referring to. They are forensic patients exactly because they have in some form or other imposed themselves onto others, whether violently or criminally or sexually. This acting upon the world does not cease because they have now been institutionalised. It continues because for these patients it cannot easily be otherwise, though it may now often be more subtle: seduction rather than sexual abuse, bullying rather than violence, passively aggressive rather than overtly controlling, inevitably pulling staff into more subtle as well as more obvious responses. This means that forensic institutions may benefit from, arguably require, access to a resource—one could say, to a mind—that is less disrupted by these dynamics and can continue to function thoughtfully on behalf of the mind, or minds, that have been disturbed. This role might be that taken up by the clinical and institutional consultant.

One of the functions most vehemently attacked by forensic patients, and hence most difficult to sustain, is thinking and reflective capacity. This may not be so difficult to understand if we think about some of the unthinkable acts of violence or perversion both perpetrated by and usually suffered by some of these patients or prisoners. We are describing patients who might be defined by their incapacity to manage their impulses and emotions psychologically, but rather to express them through the use of their own body or that of their victim. I can say that I am angry with you because I have a capacity to mentalize my emotions—to convert them into psychological states of mind which I can symbolically represent with words (Fonagy, Gergely, Jurist & Target, 2002). If I did not have this capacity, as many of our patients do not, then it is likely that the only way that I might have of expressing this same emotion and, in doing so, communicating this fact to you, is to use my body and hit you, or alternatively to harm myself and so indirectly attack you by shocking you or frightening you or distressing you. Whatever the concrete physical behaviour might be, it is its impact on the mind of the other that requires attention—something very difficult to achieve if the concrete behaviour has been particularly brutal or destructive.

One of the most extremely difficult tasks we have in working in forensic settings with very disturbed, disturbing and dangerous patients is to try to hold in mind that this acting upon others, or upon themselves, might possibly be a very primitive communication with others. In such settings, ordinary communication often fails and staff have the dual function of controlling the patient's behaviours, physical and emotional, but also taking in the emotional impact of these actions and thinking of them as potentially having symbolic meaning. If this is not kept in balance—easier said than done—there is then the danger of an oscillation between mindless and sometimes harsh discipline and control on the one hand and equally mindless sentimental sympathy and collusion on the other hand.

So what is the "psychotherapy" that might be offered to a forensic institution? Working from a psychoanalytic perspective, where we are primarily interested in unconscious processes and dynamics, our stance is that of receptive listener, curious to learn about our patient or about the work of the staff or staff group we are consulting to, and being prepared to be surprised and, with forensic patients, being prepared to be shocked, disgusted, outraged and frightened, or excited, seduced, and feeling sorry for the person. Having a conceptual framework and therapeutic model provides us with some scaffolding upon which we can locate our experiences, thoughts and feelings, as a result of which we might begin to make links and connections as we listen to and are affected by the staff describing their work with patients and with each other. Below I refer to some such scaffolding.

It is fundamental to the task of being able to manage one's emotional responses to forensic patients to have an idea about the differences in functioning between the non-psychotic and the psychotic, borderline and perverse mind. This is relevant both to an understanding of the patient's history and index offence or perversion and also to how the patient will most likely function in his or her setting.

In ordinary development, the early, unintegrated experiences and states of the infant's body and mind are gradually processed and integrated as a result of the receptive and containing relationships with primary carers. The internalisation of this good containing experience gradually leads the infant to develop his own capacity to reflect and think, to feel a sense of security, and to begin to differentiate self and other. This leads to the possibility of a sense of morality, a value system and the development of relationships (Hinshelwood, 2004).

However, if something goes wrong in this process, for example if there is insufficient or abusive or absent early parental care (containment), or if there is something inherent in the infant's predisposition so that he is not able to make use of or even rebuffs his caregivers, the capacity for containment will not be internalized. Consequently, more primitive mental processes, including splitting and projection, will remain as primary aspects of the internal world, and these will influence the person's experiences and relationships. The result is that in the emerging adult there will be little capacity for an awareness of a separate other, and therefore neither a capacity for concern for the other nor a sense of morality or a value system. In Kleinian terminology, the person remains in the paranoid schizoid way of functioning rather than having developed a capacity for more depressive position functioning. The likelihood of developing ordinary relationships is negligible.

Without the primary experience of containment, no development of a psychological self can take place, of a self that can process and think about impulses, experiences and psychological states, because such development requires the primary experience and perception of oneself, in another person's mind, as thinking and feeling (Fonagy et al, 2002). The incapacity to reflect on and integrate mental experiences results in only the body and bodily experiences being available to be used to provide a sense of relief, release or consolidation. It is not unfamiliar to hear from borderline patients about their profound sense of relief and peace following an act of violence or a suicide attempt.

The patients we are referring to are usually diagnosed as displaying severe personality disorder, psychosis or psychopathy. They have great difficulty in engaging and sustaining relationships (including therapeutic relationships). This is not so much because they don't have relationships, but more that their way of relating is to encroach on others psychologically, affecting the balance of the minds of both, for example, through physical action or violence, sexually perverse behaviour or self-harm. Whether it is any of these actions or even if it is only words that are used, the function of this is to act upon the other's mind in an intrusive way.

The more disturbed patient, therefore, is very likely to be relating in a manner which includes the greater use of powerful processes of splitting (more accurately, fragmentation) and projection, and other primitive processes. As a result, he is likely to unconsciously use people around him, patients and staff, through processes of projection, to represent parts of his disturbed and disturbing internal world, if not actually to act it out. It can be said that borderline, personality disordered and perverse patients act on their environment as a way of expelling parts of their unbearable internal world. This results in the recreation in the current situation of dynamics and interactions similar to those experienced in earlier childhood.

If the patient has not ever been the object in the mind of another (a carer or parent), then he does not have a sense of a space in his own mind which he can occupy and use to think in. As a result, he is likely to project different parts of his mind into whatever space he is in and affect those around him who are also occupying that space. This is the way in which forensic patients impact in gross or more subtle ways on those around them. However, this creates the possibility for the practitioner to understand aspects of the patient's internal world, if we can be receptive enough to their projections, come to recognise them in ourselves and in our colleagues and in our interactions, and be capable of reflecting on their nature and functioning. The enormous problem, though, is that the splitting and fragmentation requires an acute capacity by the staff to relate to and—crucially—link up the various aspects of the patient's presentation. Working from their own experiences of the patient, both as an individual and as a member of the ward he is in, is essential in forensic settings. The role of the consultant is to try to create the space to do this and to begin to see the possible links and connections.

It is very useful to have the concept of what we might think of as a vertical split in the personality of a perverse and violent patient, a split which differentiates the more violent and perverse part of the personality from the non-perverse part (Chasseguet-Smirgel, 1985). This vertical structure can be thought of as if superimposed on the more familiar horizontal structure differentiating neurotic from borderline and from psychotic parts of the personality. One of the important ways in which this is useful is to remind us that some patients who are diagnosed with psychiatric illness might well be aided by the use of anti-psychotic medication and significantly reduce their psychotic presentation and ideation, but there will probably remain in place a disordered personality which was responsible for the index offence and which has probably been traumatized by the fact of committing that offence.

In thinking about forensic patients it is very useful to have in mind what is fundamental about forensic patients—to recognise the aggression, hostility and malevolence inherent in their offending behaviours. This is obvious with overtly violent patients, but it is equally true of patients who act out in sexually perverse and sado-masochistic ways. The apparently sexual behavior is recruited in the service of aggression, and the patients themselves, as well as the victims, are affected by this violence and hostility, certainly in their minds and, in the case of masochistic or suicidal patients, sometimes in their bodies. Robert Stoller, an American psychiatrist and psychoanalyst, refers to sexual perversion as the "erotic form of hatred" (1975).

Understanding this hostility and violence is fundamental to understanding the forensic patient. One of the central ways in which this hostility is enacted, other than physically upon others, is in its impact on the patient's capacity to use his mind, and especially the destruction of the capacity to think and be sensitive to others. The fundamental task, in my view, of the mental health institutions is to take very great care of the mental states of the mental health staff. This requires a sophisticated but essential understanding of the nature of work with forensic and personality disordered patients which is not always present in our contemporary institutions. Hinshelwood discusses this very powerfully in his book *Suffering Insanity* (2004).

If the original family environment was one in which attachment figures expressed depressive or narcissistic anxiety, or aggression, or sexual or physical abuse towards the child, the child would not only have been deprived of the caregiver's reflective and thinking mind as a model for developing his own, but may have learned to actively avoid thinking about his own and/or others' experiences because they were disturbing or violent. As a consequence, there is little likelihood of the development of a sense of a real other person, and therefore no system of values or moral code. Callousness will emerge as a way of functioning, an apparently total lack of sensitivity which is actually rooted in anxiety. Only a sense of triumph or dominance over the external world or the immediate attention or unquestioning admiration of others provides any sense of safety or relief (Hinshelwood, 2004). Intermingled with this there is likely to be the disrupting core complex anxiety about both closeness (which results in feelings of claustrophobia) and separateness (which results in feelings of agoraphobia), and a resultant sense of agitation which can be very disturbing both to the individual himself and to those around him (Glasser, 1984).

Patients in a high-security setting, usually because of the nature of their developmental history and experiences, are likely to have a very disordered reaction to care. Such patients are characterised by constant attacks on and often defeat of help. This defeat may be by aggressively dismissive means or, more often, by corrupting the help. This is likely to be based in part on their personal experience of caregivers being abusive and violent or sexually perverse. This often results in one of the most difficult aspects of what is required by the practitioner in a forensic setting. The sense of good work and of the patient "getting better", probably desired by all clinicians, is often absent for long periods of time, and if this is not understood as being part of the patient's symptoms then it can be very demoralising.

For the patient who has little if any trust in others, identification with the aggressor becomes a likely defensive posture. This is an especially acute issue when, by definition, a secure institution is struggling to provide both care and custody. There may be unconscious pressure for both care and control to be corrupted—care might become indulgence and complacency and control might become mindless and sadistic—or alternatively, the difficult tension of care or the control is lost, with the result of perversely providing just one or the other (Hinshelwood, 2004). It is interesting to speculate whether this is in part an enactment of the patient's earlier relationships to the parental couple, who were experienced as narcissistic, perverse and corrupt, or as violent (or both), or as lacking a capacity for co-operation and not displaying a mix of maternal and paternal functions.

As well as enacting these functions of care and control of the patients, forensic institutions might also inadvertently institutionalise their patient. The long-term care of forensic patients in medium and high security, for example, may not infrequently result in their desocialisation—a type of "social illness" emerges (Main, 1989), resulting from their dependency not only on the doctors and nurses but less consciously on the structures, boundaries and containment offered by being within the physical and emotional framework of the institution. Adaptation to the particular nature of the hospital regime and the hospital staff may be counterproductive as far as learning to live in lower security or outside the hospital is concerned. Hence, part of the task of the staff is paradoxically to protect their patients from the hospital system itself. This is, however, no easy task, as the staff themselves are also likely to be dependent to a certain degree on a parallel set of physical and emotional safeguards which, quite properly, they require to support and sustain themselves in their work.

The fate of those working with violent patients is to feel frightened or violated or sadistic; the fate of those working with sexually perverse patients is to feel corrupted and seduced or disgusted; the fate of those working with personality disordered patients is to feel abused or omnipotently indulgent or hostile and dismissive. Staff in high-security settings work with a range of patients who are likely to be all of the above: violent, sexually perverse and personality disordered. As a result, the institution is likely to be flooded, and the staff overwhelmed, by fear, violation, corruption, seduction and abuse. Or—usually and—they may feel defensively sadistic, dismissively disgusted and abusive (directly or indirectly by, for example, being unrealistically/omnipotently indulgent and hence "betraying" the patient). Without the opportunity to reflect on these inevitable and very difficult experiences, the staff working in forensic institutions are destined to repeat the early corrupt, mindless and depriving experiences that most forensic patients had in their beginnings. If staff can sustain a thinking capacity, then in doing so they provide a psychological setting within which some patients might be able to take the first tentative steps from acting out their internal worlds to beginning to be able to reflect on themselves and on their relating to others, and so to begin to develop a less disturbed and disturbing way of functioning.

Acknowledgement

I would like to express my profound gratitude to all the colleagues at Ashworth Hospital with whom I learned more than I can ever fully acknowledge.

I would also like to express my thanks to Dr Rob Hale, Consultant Psychiatrist in Psychotherapy at the Portman Clinic, who, over a number of years, generously shared with me his extensive knowledge and experience of consulting to institutions.

CHAPTER SIX

Interpersonal dynamics in the everyday practice of a forensic unit

Gabriel Kirtchuk, David Reiss and John Gordon

We are clinicians working within a large medium-secure hospital in the United Kingdom. The service comprises both acute and rehabilitation wards, as well as a high dependency unit and an on-site hostel. In this chapter we will discuss how we have introduced to our clinical practice a method of exploring interpersonal dynamics in a systematic and integrated way.

We aim to enhance and improve clinical communication. It is an everyday finding that routine clinical meetings in our unit, such as ward rounds, tend predominantly to comprise discussion along behavioural and symptomatic lines, and we believe that this is probably true of many other similar settings as well. Of course these perspectives are essential, but they do not provide information about the subtleties of interpersonal communication between patient and all members of staff from which it may be possible to explore the nature of the patient's internal world, as well as the underlying dynamics of the index offence.

In the multidisciplinary context of our work there is an increasing tendency for the different professions to organize their clinical interventions separately and to employ different languages, with limited overlap and a restricted range of conceptual possibilities. Beyond the effects of major socio-political changes regarding professional roles, and therefore identities (for example, CSIP/NIMHE et al., 2005), we present two other underlying explanations for this lack of institutional integration. First, the professions may tend to fragment as a result of behaviour that results from the projection of our patients' fragmented minds, so that there is an active process by which not only individual members of the multidisciplinary team but the separate professions are differentially perceived, used, valued or devalued by patients. Second, all organizations struggle with the ongoing requirement to define and to stick to the primary task(s): the work that they have been set up and authorized to do. In order to achieve this, there is a fundamental requirement to be in touch with the reality of the work, and in forensic settings this reality is extraordinarily painful and frightening. Consequently, at an institutional level, group defences ("social defences": see Jaques, 1955; Menzies, 1960; and Hinshelwood, 1987b) are mobilized to shield members of the organization from the emotional impact of contact with patients.

To overcome all these inescapable centrifugal forces, we believe it is vital that each clinical team develops a specific framework to organize its clinical practice so that fissural tendencies can be monitored and addressed. Specifically, the different professionals involved in a patient's care must meet regularly to coordinate their separate views based on certain shared concepts and a common language. By doing this, all staff, even if they come from different theoretical backgrounds, can work in partnership to interpret and understand the observed behaviour of the patients.

The method we use, which is described below, is able to reveal the underlying dynamics of a patient's interactions in a way that can be understood and contributed to by all multidisciplinary team members. The vast majority of those under our care display psychotic symptoms on admission, and the most common diagnosis is schizophrenia. Although treatment-resistant illnesses are not uncommon, most patients eventually respond relatively well to medication, the therapeutic milieu and the psychological therapies they receive, with a consequent decline of florid symptoms and an associated reduction in overt offensive and dangerous behaviour. However, in many cases their undercurrent motivations, as well as the disturbed relational patterns involved in the offending behaviour, are still active and are being acted out in their relationships with the various team members. Our approach is able to scrutinise the patient's interpersonal relationships, and involves examination of four interpersonal perspectives, including how the patient experiences others (transference) and how others experience themselves in their interaction with the patient (countertransference).

Objectivity, which is seen as the gold standard of scientific measurement, is prized and promoted in modern clinical practice, whereas subjective experience, which has traditionally been viewed as not meeting the criterion of detachment, has consequently been marginalised in many aspects of psychiatric and psychological discourse. What we are proposing is that subjective experience, in particular the way that staff react to patients, can be codified, organised, and contextualised so as to make it a valid and reliable tool in routine clinical work. We believe that accurate appraisal of interpersonal dynamics, when used in association with risk assessment and risk monitoring, forms a sensitive radar which may not only help detect the early warning signs of problems, but can also provide staff with insight into a patient's functioning. The process of determining the dynamics will improve the shared understanding of a patient's problems, and has the potential to lead to an intervention which can help head off potential challenging or violent behaviour. We believe that it is helpful and important to include and integrate this assessment of the interpersonal dynamics (ID) into everyday clinical practice.

Theoretical background

Risk assessments give lists of risk factors but do not tell you how to implement treatment programmes when progress is blocked due to a patient's repetitive and counterproductive pattern of behaviour. ID gives insight into the underlying dynamics, and once these are formulated, an intervention can be developed and implemented which takes account of them. In many cases understanding of the dynamics is itself sufficient as an intervention because this supports the integration of the staff team in their work with the patient.

An understanding of interpersonal behaviour is a fundamental prerequisite of psychodynamic diagnosis, as dysfunctional patterns underlie the formation and maintenance of many problems which are a part of mental disorder. Benjamin (1996) has outlined how psychotherapists have tried to develop a more objective understanding of psychopathology in interpersonal terms. Her Structural Analysis of Social Behaviour (SASB) model derives from the pioneering theoretical work of Harry Stack Sullivan (1953) and the empirical study of Henry Murray (1938). Murray produced a list of fundamental human needs, a selection of which were arranged by Timothy Leary (1957) around two perpendicular axes to form a circle, a type of arrangement now known as a circumplex (Guttman, 1966). Circumplex models have a horizontal axis, with love and hate as the opposing polarities, and a vertical axis which ranges from dominance to submission. Schaefer (1965) proposed a vertical axis, modelled on parenting behaviours, which is defined in terms of allowing autonomy versus control. Circular models of these types have been validated by empirical research (Schaefer, 1965; Wiggins 1882). In the forensic context, Blackburn (1998) has used the interpersonal circle to examine the relationship between interpersonal style and criminality in both mentally ill and personality disordered patients.

What is the best way to determine, in the setting of an inpatient forensic psychiatry unit, how our patients and staff experience their interpersonal relations? The Operationalized Psychodynamic Diagnostics (OPD) Task Force (2001) have formulated a reliable empirical method to determine stable but dysfunctional patterns in relationships. It took up the circumplex model, was heavily influenced by the SASB (Benjamin, 1996), and has modified this approach by taking into account the work of others who have also outlined methods of observing personal interactions (Luborsky & Crits-Christoph, 1990; Weiss & Sampson, 1986; Horowitz, 1991; Hoffmann & Gill, 1988; Strupp & Binder, 1984). Furthermore, OPD includes, within an objective framework and methodology, two fundamental aspects of psychoanalytic object relations theory which are crucial in order for staff to understand the interpersonal dynamic dimension as dramatized on the ward.

First, psychoanalytic object relations theory proposes that the infant (subject) relates to others (objects) at least from birth (and probably before as well), and that development towards maturity depends on the vicissitudes and integration of repeated subject-object interactions. The key point is that far more is going on in interpersonal interactions than that which is objectively observable from outside the relationship. The subject brings to (even imposes upon) the relationship needs, anxieties and intense feelings of love as well as hate, and consequently may experience an interaction totally differently from the report of an external observer. Also, based on this subjective evaluation—conscious *and* unconscious—a residue or template of relating is established within the subject's mind: self relating to object under the aegis of a particular emotion (Kernberg, 1980). The idea that we carry around schemas, maps or scenarios of expected, feared or longed for relationships is not unique to psychoanalysis. However, the finding that the unconscious deployment of these internal self-object relationships is ubiquitous and may allow very little of the externally observable qualities of the interaction to register, especially when the subject's internal world includes multiple, intensely contradictory and incompatible versions of self (selves) relating to object(s), is a central psychoanalytic contribution.

Second, complementing the hypothesis of interacting internal and external worlds of self-object relationships, is the insight that one pattern of self relating to object may be used unconsciously to obscure, deflect or evade altogether the emergence of another. For example, Ezriel (1959) proposed that in any clinical interaction, it is useful to consider how the patient compulsively seeks to establish a "required relationship" in order to prevent the emergence of an "avoided relationship", which in turn is believed to usher in an overwhelming "calamitous relationship". Thus, a forensic patient who repeatedly complies and shows respectful deference and idealization towards staff (required) may fear the outbreak of conflicts and bitter anger (avoided) which he is convinced would lead to chaotic feelings of persecution, depersonalization and loss of control: "murder" of self and/or object (calamitous). Hinshelwood (1992), in the context of psychodynamic assessment and formulation, also takes up the extent to which past and present, "there and then" and "here and now" internalized and external relationship prototypes conflict or harmonize with one another. He is particularly sensitive to the patient's "point of maximum pain" (calamitous relationship) and how other relationship scripts in the patient's repertoire may be evoked as defences against that mental pain.

The totality of OPD is a comprehensive, structured assessment protocol which combines descriptive phenomenological diagnostics (ICD-10, DSM-IV) with psychodynamic features derived from psychoanalysis. Patients are assessed on five axes: (I) experience of illness and prerequisites for treatment, (II) interpersonal relations, (III) conflicts, (IV) structure, and (V) mental and psychosomatic disorders. In our work with the multidisciplinary team, we concentrate on the framework that underlies Axis II, which concerns the transference-countertransference configurations enacted between each patient and those members of staff involved in his treatment as they are experienced every day on the ward. The basic procedure is to conceptualize aspects of the patient's core relationship patterns by (1) clarifying how the patient characteristically experiences himself and the other in interaction with himself, and (2) describing how the other (staff member) usually experiences the patient as well as him/herself in their interactions. From this material it is possible to hypothesize the significant internalized object relationships of the patient and the manner in which they may influence external relationships on the ward. Most importantly, team members are provided with a means to validate the meaning of their emotional responses; to compare and explore them with colleagues; and to develop a cross-disciplinary language which, whatever particular professionals' distinctive tasks, allows communication about interpersonal relationships with patients to be a shared focus of clinical work.

The project

How have we implemented our method in routine clinical practice? Our team has introduced a regular weekly clinical discussion, lasting up to an hour, during which we discuss the interpersonal dynamics (ID) of the patient based on the OPD Axis II. These ID meetings are alternated with risk assessment and monitoring meetings, using the HCR-20 (Webster et al, 1997) and START (Webster et al, 2004) instruments. The meeting is attended by the multidisciplinary team members, who have been on the ward round which just precedes it, and takes place in three stages. The initial part is a presentation of background information; next we discuss the interpersonal dynamics; and finally we review the management strategy.

The first part of the meeting takes approximately ten minutes. In this, the patient's background history is summarised, particularly emphasising early interpersonal relationships with parental figures and siblings and continuing with relevant information about interpersonal relationships in adulthood. The index offence is also outlined, including its nature, the background circumstances, the dates and the medico-legal outcome. Then an overview of the current pattern of interpersonal relations is presented, with an emphasis on the current difficulties in case management.

In the next and longest part of the meeting, which lasts 30–40 minutes, the group members are invited to go through the four interpersonal dimensions specified by OPD Axis II on the basis of the information already available to them about the patient. The team identifies as many items as possible on the interpersonal circle (the items are listed on a form for Axis II of the OPD) which describe the patient's relationship patterns, and then makes a more rigorous selection of those which are the most prominent. For each item listed, the evidence is recorded. On the basis of this refined sample, the group attempts to make a dynamic formulation of the dysfunctional pattern of interactions which includes the "here and now" (on the ward), early development, adult life and the interpersonal nature of the index offence. The overall aim is the identification of maladaptive or collusive patterns of relatedness in which the staff get "caught up" unwillingly, reinforcing the patient's destructive behavioural pattern.

The final part of the meeting, which takes about 10–20 minutes, is a discussion about the change of strategy that can be adopted by the different disciplines with regard to their own interactions with the patient.

Our discussions encourage the full participation and involvement of all members of staff. During a meeting about interpersonal dynamics, everyone present who has had involvement with the patient is invited to discuss their different viewpoints of the interpersonal relationships on the basis of their experience of him/her in their respective clinical roles. Therefore, the formulation of the interpersonal dynamics is carried out by the totality of the staff rather than being the reflection of one "specialist" from the outside providing a report. Different members of staff may evoke contrasting patterns of interaction, depending on their role and/or personal characteristics. The elucidation of the patterns of interrelationship offers a way to address difficulties which are sometimes experienced at the managerial level with the patient, or involve entanglements of repetitive and difficult behaviour between staff and patients, e.g. splitting between staff, difficulties in setting clear boundaries, etc.

A vitally important advantage of working in the professional group setting is the possibility for colleagues to identify in one another behaviours and responses which may indicate underlying attitudes and feelings towards patients. People may sometimes find it very difficult to identify or acknowledge their own emotional responses, but can more easily see and decode the observed behaviour and comments of others. While sometimes, particularly initially, this process can be uncomfortable, over time group members come to value that others can be more aware of feelings of which one is unaware oneself.

Information gathered in this way is integrated, used in the care plan, and can be revisited on a regular basis. The formulation derived from sustained attention to the interpersonal dynamics can also inform the work of different professionals who are providing specific therapeutic interventions, providing them with a framework for an overall strategy, so they are more aware of conflicts, incoherence and complementarities within the team's approach to particular patients. We are currently negotiating with management and the leaders of all the professional disciplines to ensure that every team in our hospital unit has some method of communicating information about risk and interpersonal dynamics with its members.

In the following examples, items on the four perspectives (how the patient repeatedly experiences others, how the patient repeatedly experiences himself, how others experience the patient, how others experience themselves) which are listed in the OPD Axis II are indicated by *italics*. These two cases are fictitious, but they are based on cases the authors have assessed and treated over a prolonged period of time and in different institutions.

Case example 1

Lee is a male patient, now in his early forties, who was admitted to the medium-secure unit several years ago. He is short and stocky, with coarse features as well as facial scarring, walks in an ungainly manner, and wears shabby clothes. He had received a hospital order subsequent to his index offence, which involved loitering near a children's paddling pool in possession of a small axe. At this time he reported sadistic and sexual fantasies towards young children, including chopping them up. On initial assessment in hospital he had manifested psychotic symptoms characteristic of schizophrenia, and he was subsequently treated with antipsychotic medication. Psychological assessment of his personality had also revealed traits of various personality disorders, predominantly antisocial and borderline.

Lee's history showed that his parents had separated soon after his birth when his father had been forced to undergo "re-education" during the Chinese Cultural Revolution. He was subsequently brought up by his mother and an alcohol and drug abusing step-father who physically assaulted his mother, his siblings and Lee himself.

The meeting to assess his interpersonal dynamics was attended by the consultant, the junior doctor, the primary nurse, the psychologist and the consultant psychotherapist. Other members of the team were unavailable. The junior doctor presented the background history, including the above details. She also noted that although Lee had made slow progress during this admission, whenever he began to be given more responsibility and increasing freedom, his psychosis relapsed. He would then tell staff that he was afraid to disclose his symptoms in case it set back his progress. Recently, subsequent to the anniversary of the death of an aunt with whom he had a close relationship, Lee was observed to have become more depressed and withdrawn. The nurse noted that his current presentation was that he appeared to be isolated and unmotivated, spending most of the time in his room. He also reported that the patient sometimes became very anxious and complained about testicular pain, particularly when it was late at night. At these times he would demand that the nursing staff call the on-call junior doctor immediately to attend to the problem. The psychologist reported that he engaged very well in treatment and did not stress his offending behaviour; rather, he emphasized Lee's view that he was a victim of circumstances. The consultant reported that at his recent tribunal Lee had expressed the wish to be discharged and indicated that his presentation at ward rounds was that he usually made a lot of requests and often appeared to make little effort to organise things for himself.

With this information we began to explore how we believed that the patient experienced others. The way the patient presented at ward rounds, often making demands for others to allow him to do things which he felt he was prevented from doing, was seen as indicating that he experienced others as *controlling* him. The way he made these requests, as though he felt he was being neglected by staff, was seen as showing that he felt others were *ignoring* him. His family history and current presentation also indicated that he perceived others as *attacking* and *rejecting* him.

Prior to his tribunal, the patient himself had reported to staff that he felt safe to be in the outside world, but to be sure that he would not harm others he would need to live in an isolated place in the countryside, far from any children. This was taken to indicate that he experienced himself as *attacking and threatening,* and that he also saw himself as *fleeing* from others. His requests on the ward round for more independence, as well as his demands for freedom, indicated that he perceived himself as *stressing his own autonomy.* Whether Lee was capable of experiencing the inevitable tension which would arise from a simultaneous awareness that he continued to be a dangerous person and required liberty is uncertain, but staff did struggle with this contradiction.

Accordingly, staff on the ward saw Lee as *attacking and threatening* because of the nature of his index offence, his lack of responsibility for himself, and his physical appearance. They saw his presentation on the ward round and at other times—for example, when he was ill he would demand to see a doctor immediately for minor problems—as *making claims and demands* and *controlling* them. His current isolation (his "freedom far from others" on the ward) was seen as *secluding* himself and consequently preventing potentially constructive contacts which might moderate his destructiveness.

At one level, in response to these conflicting images of Lee, team members experienced themselves in their interaction with him in correspondingly unintegrated ways. The psychologist believed that he was *helping and caring* for Lee; nurses and doctors on the contrary saw themselves as *giving up, resigned* and also as *rejecting* and *ignoring* him. In fact, at a deeper level, the latter was agreed to be the gut response by everyone on initial meeting with this patient.

Having completed our survey of the interpersonal dimensions, we try to relate them to one another. Lee feels others to be controlling, attacking and abandoning: *they* are dangerous. He responds to these perceptions by stressing his own autonomy, threatening and fleeing from others; *he* then becomes dangerous. Clearly, his responses can be considered as counter-reactions: control triggers autonomy, threat evokes aggression and abandonment leads to flight, all in the service of self-protection. But there is also a mirroring aspect, as Lee shows staff through his treatment of them how he feels they relate to him. Consequently, however, some staff members see him as simply controlling, some see him as dangerous, but others feel that he is a victim. In reaction to such confusingly intractable vicious cycles of mutual attribution, staff members either attempt to extricate themselves by adopting only one of the perspectives; or, exhausted by prolonged attempts to resolve the contradictions, they resort to rejecting Lee and give up. Ultimately, even those members of staff who want to care for him come to experience Lee's repetitive dysfunctional use of care (such as calling the doctor late at night) as provocative teasing, and they too reject him.

What seems to be enacted by Lee and his team is a scenario in which the fundamental forensic tasks of control and care, as they are expressed in the numerous role-specific acts of providing structure (appropriate autonomy) and showing concern that staff ordinarily perform for patients, become radically distorted. By submitting to his regular urgent requests for attention to his physical symptoms late at night, the otherwise available but rejected caring offered by doctors is perverted. For not only does Lee require that they carry out an intimate examination, but through the timing of his importuning he persistently disrupts other patients' sleep and the nurses' shift, and invades the doctors' rest as well. When the staff members realize how their concern (love), as well as their autonomy, is undermined, they inevitably want to reject or ignore him in order to dissociate themselves from participation in an uncomfortable exploitation of their wishes to help. Unfortunately, withdrawal—both in disgust and in order to assist Lee to gain control (structure and autonomy) over his impulse to repeat abuse or being abused (his dangerousness)—may confirm, once again, the story of his life: his parents ignored or rejected him.

A further consequence of this oscillation between collusion with an exciting enactment and subsequent feelings of rejection and revulsion towards the patient is that Lee's most painful, underlying depression—a result of all the losses in his life which the anniversary of the death of his aunt links up again with the early traumas of the parental separation, neglect and abuse—is disregarded. Staff members do not just feel like rejecting Lee (in the countertransference) but in fact abandon this part of the patient. Alternatively, by *adjusting and submitting* to Lee through passive compliance with his demands for "care", whether in the form of dysfunctional observations (permitting him to go out and thus ignoring the risk he poses), in allowing him to dictate the length of his stay in the unit by rejecting interventions (secluding himself), or by *giving up resigned* on him through active rejection or neglect (non-recognition) of his suffering, staff obscure one of Lee's basic anxieties. This is that he feels overwhelmingly scared to be discharged from the unit because it is unconsciously reminiscent of an early form of abandonment. By activating the abusive, maladaptive relationship, what is avoided again is addressing the neglected child in him. He ends up re-enacting the sado-masochistic relationship with his stepfather. Further, staff members could consider the hypothesis that the index offence itself was a re-enactment of the identical traumas, with the difference that he himself was the perpetrator rather than the victim of the abuse. The conclusion, in terms of the clinical discussion, is that what should be addressed is the loss of the object and what it would mean for him to actually leave the unit. For this, one has to create a more functional relationship with Lee—to work on separation—before any actual separation, which is currently premature.

What emerged in the conversation between team members involved in Lee's treatment was the chronic difficulty of him being stuck as long as his unbearable separation anxieties, amounting to fears of annihilation, remained ignored. Gradually the faint background voice of his depression in response to the anniversary could be heard. By becoming more aware of the total interpersonal dynamic dimension the staff could begin to recover a sense of their own caring values, and the patient benefits from the possibility of his depression being finally addressed. Lee, who for so long has been neglecting himself, is no longer also neglected by the staff when they can hold a more complete picture of him in their minds.

Case example 2

Bridget is in her late twenties and was raised in a small, rural Irish village. There were numerous siblings, but the chronically embattled, violent parents were not only unable to care for their children but exposed them to their intense conflicts. A slightly older cousin was experienced by Bridget as caring, although the state of general deprivation was so extensive that often the children did not have enough to eat. Eventually the parents separated, and Bridget was sent to a great uncle who treated her cruelly. In an attempt to become independent, Bridget followed her cousin, who had come to England some years before. She seemed to have sufficient awareness to know that she badly needed help, and contacted a psychologist, with whom she began to meet. However, Bridget deteriorated and was referred to her local psychiatric service, where she was diagnosed with a psychotic illness. She subsequently made a number of attempts to form relationships with women, but was never able to enjoy a sexual relationship except with a much older woman, whom she met and moved in with at a time when the woman's longstanding female partner was in hospital. After the partner returned, Bridget felt rejected, and this precipitated another relapse and the index offence, when Bridget threatened her lover with a broken bottle. She was then admitted to a regional secure unit.

In our interpersonal dynamics meeting were present the consultant psychiatrist, art therapist, consultant psychologist, occupational therapist, junior doctor and the consultant psychotherapist. Unfortunately, the primary nurse was unable to attend. The junior doctor presented the above history. The consultant psychiatrist conveyed that the team was considering how to plan Bridget's future treatment, and mentioned in particular an insistent request of the patient to be referred to a particular, extremely specialised psychological therapy unit at the Maudsley Hospital. The psychologist remarked that in spite of a multiplicity of interventions by the psychology department, very little if any change had been noted apart from a brief and limited focus on anger management. The art therapist, in contrast, spoke about the vivid and rich imagery during her sessions with Bridget. The occupational therapist once again referred to the regular disparity between Bridget's apparent promise of mature sophistication and her actual achievements, which were mediocre. These comments indicated a prevailing perception of Bridget as suffering from a very persistent and chronic mental illness on the one hand, while displaying a seeming psychological-mindedness and capacity for insight on the other. In fact, during her time as an inpatient, Bridget had evidenced a remarkable capacity to elicit staff efforts to provide her with an enormous range of therapeutic interventions.

A second theme which emerged in the discussion concerned Bridget's apparent sexual voraciousness, which both the clinical psychologist and the art therapist mentioned. The psychologist said, for example, that Bridget had asked whether the staff could provide her with a "Sybian" (a mechanical device designed to assist female sexual arousal) in order to increase her gratification. And in line with the usual attempt to respond to this patient's needs, this request was being given serious consideration.

According to the interpersonal dynamic perspectives, the patient largely experiences others on whom she depends and under whose care she is as either *controlling* or *abandoning* her, while some other figures are experienced as *greatly helping, caring and protecting* (cousin and psychologist in the past). She perceives herself, in response, as *stressing her own autonomy* as well as *admiring and idealising* her own capacity to decide what she needs and who can provide that for her. Also, she acknowledges being *accusing* and *attacking*, but she justifies this on the basis of old grievances, particularly if she feels that somebody else gets something to which she feels she is entitled.

Members of staff experience her as leaning on and *clinging* to them but also as *making claims and demands* in an *attacking and threatening* manner. In response, they experience themselves as *greatly wanting to help*, sometimes in an idealised way, while at the same time *crouching and devaluing themselves*. In the end they tend to *give up*, feeling empty and *resigned*.

This interpersonal pattern only confirms Bridget's life experience of being left in a very impoverished world, as whatever is offered does not seem to be either good enough or appropriate for her to be fed and to grow. The staff tend to get caught up in two main states of mind, either wanting to provide something very special for her following her own idealisations (being suitable for a specialised programme in a highly prestigious institution) or feeling deflated and depleted as if not having anything worthwhile to offer her. The first is a narcissistic state in which the patient's "sophisticated capacities" are responded to by staff convinced that they can find the ideally effective treatment. Culminating in the request for the "Sybian", this state can be seen for what it is: the patient's "perfect solution" is to be provided with an instrument capable of satisfying all her needs without having to depend on a human relationship. The effect of colluding with this fantasy and its collapse leaves staff depleted, convinced that in reality they have nothing of value to offer; even more, that there is no patient with whom they could establish an appropriate partnership. In this respect members of staff become symbolically equated with the older woman who is deprived of her partner and enables Bridget to step in to fill the vacuum. When these totally unrealistic convictions disintegrate, she believes that she has been once again violently rejected and robbed of nurturance and this, in turn, triggers her own threats and attacks on the staff and patients on the ward, as happened in a potentially fatal manner in her index offence. Interestingly enough, this dynamic also seems to reflect the phenomenological psychiatric diagnosis of schizoaffective disorder: manic self- and object idealization incessantly alternates with persecuting emptiness.

The recommendation would be for the staff to be mindful of not getting caught up in either idealised or devalued images; to make an independent assessment, released from the spell of omnipotent and controlling projections; and to re-establish and maintain a professional intercourse between themselves based on managing their tendency to participate in vicious cycles with the patient. In particular, staff members should accordingly be better able to bear the depressive realities of Bridget's illness and of their own limitations, losses which she cannot tolerate, without swings between manic attempts to repair and total feelings of uselessness.

Conclusion

We have outlined how we have integrated psychodynamic working into the clinical practice of a busy multidisciplinary forensic psychiatry team by giving staff a framework through which they can productively use information, which otherwise might not be shared, to improve their understanding of important clinical issues. The Interpersonal Dynamics meeting follows a set format but allows people to be spontaneous within it, not reliant on written "professional" reports, as they compare their views on the various perspectives. The material which emerges is often in response to the comments of others, and a lively discussion frequently results. Information gathered is put into the required format as the meeting progresses.

This method is very accessible. All members of staff are able to understand the four perspectives and make a contribution using the outline sheets provided, which contain all the vocabulary required. However, a relatively high degree of familiarity with the theoretical background, as well as extensive experience in psychodynamic work, is required of the psychotherapist who supports the group, and who is thus able to both create a safe atmosphere for staff to divulge their innermost feelings about the patient and facilitate a full formulation which takes these revelations out of the realm of the personal and places them fully in a professional mental health context. If team members understand the dysfunctional dynamics which may be present, and are able to place them in the context of the patient's life, index offence and level of risk, a vital step in promoting a collaborative treatment project which is both therapeutic and safe has been taken.

CONCLUSION:

The role of a psychotherapy department in the large forensic service

John Gordon and Gabriel Kirtchuk

Context

The title of this concluding chapter refers to and acknowledges Hinshelwood's paper which has informed our orientation to the work presented in this book. In "The Psychotherapist's Role in a Large Psychiatric Institution" (1987a), he describes how ubiquitous, large, inter- and intra-group dynamics within psychiatric hospitals affect—pervasively because unconsciously—participating professionals' perceptions and experience of their own, as well as of others', roles and identities. Applying the concept of the "social defence system" (Jaques, 1955; Menzies, 1960), Hinshelwood emphasizes the intrinsic emotional burden for individual members of staff whose work, whatever their particular responsibilities, is an encounter with madness. Each individually must develop means to cope with the real and the phantasy (subjective and unconscious) implications of contact with people who both display and evoke states of mindlessness, alienation and the threat of spinning out of control: "It is a fear of personal annihilation/fragmentation, and is connected with the psychotic's obliteration of his mind and his reality, internal and external" (1987a, pp. 209–210).

As an organized group, however, staff collectively elaborate further protective supports to alleviate the lonely psychological struggle of the individual to survive the intense anxieties posed by the nature of the work: the social defence system. Methods of doing the job (mechanical routines, depersonalizing technical procedures, training in treatment "techniques"), as well as mutually generated perceptions of one's own and other professional groups, can be devised, enlisted and enacted unconsciously by the group to bolster its members' individual defences. By providing group-sanctioned patterns of relating to patients, other staff and managers which suppress any potentially disturbing contacts, especially between staff and patients, the work is systematically regulated to such a degree that anxiety is either kept to a minimum or distributed around the organization—as far from one's department or ward as possible. But as Hinshelwood makes clear, such safety through distancing is achieved at the cost of deadening all interactions with patients which might become lively, and therefore emotionally disconcerting. Not only patients but the staff as well can be rendered institutionalized as a consequence of their own group-level hidden agenda to reduce mental turbulence.

One consequence of these unconscious processes and interactions is that the capacity of staff to carry out the professional work of their organization is jeopardized. How is it possible to work with patients if engagement with them is a source of dread? They can only be "treated" at a distance, and many courses and training sessions are made available to teach staff emotionally disconnected "techniques" for such long-distance interaction with their patients. At the extreme, most of the effort is devoted to defending from emotional contact-contamination (viewed as inseparable) and becomes anti-task, however unaware staff may be of this relentless diversion of resources.

On the other hand, few staff remain altogether oblivious of the impact on their work of their joint, unconsciously defensive operations. Feelings of dissatisfaction, frustration and impotence, at times even utter hopelessness, invade the working day. Although these painful emotional experiences are usually blamed on the difficult patients, the unsupportive management or the general political situation, occasionally staff feel worried that they are not doing the job well. Concern can take the form of a fear of being found out and attacked—audited, investigated or "cut" for example—which in turn may trigger protective retaliation by casting aspersion or blame on some other group in the hospital. Alternatively, internal states of unworthiness and guilt may overwhelm a staff member's esteem and sense of purpose. Illness, absences, burn-out and drop-out can follow; or the morale of an entire professional group declines.

Hinshelwood's most original contribution is to consider the phantasy role of the psychotherapist in the context of the hospital social defence system: ". . . the significant point about the psychotherapist in the institution is that he represents, with his special form of treatment, a fostering of human contact and human relations . . . I want to suggest that the psychotherapist is felt, unconsciously, to represent for the hospital some sense of its lost life, humanity and organization" (1987a, p. 212). As a result, the psychotherapist is either condemned and devalued as a container of the dreaded contact with madness or put on a pedestal—idealized—as the embodiment of the denied, attacked yearning for integrated relationships. From either position, at the organizational level the psychotherapist can never be used to help contribute to the real task, for no creative link can be established by other professional colleagues with a feared and hated or exalted figure. Distance as defence, pervading the whole organization, not surprisingly also envelops the (non-)relationship to the psychotherapist, whose interventions in turn may unconsciously collude with these distorted, polarized images or fail to consider their defensive use by other members of the organization.

The work we have presented in this book, and the fundamental orientating concept we have chosen—the countertransference—express our response to the dilemmas Hinshelwood explores. What could be the role of a Forensic Psychotherapy Department in the forensic setting, and how can the inevitable, unconscious institutional dynamics be navigated? Hinshelwood ends his analysis by stating that ". . . we may sometimes find some ways of creating dialogues about the work and about relations between groups in the psychiatric service which do not end up by reinforcing projective distortions of each other" (1987a, p. 215). In this chapter we review how we have tackled this challenge in order to propose a possible direction for the work of consultant forensic psychotherapists and other colleagues in Forensic Psychotherapy Departments.

Forensic anxiety

The patients whom staff encounter in forensic settings do not only suffer from and evoke in staff complementary anxieties of contamination by madness. The whole diagnostic spectrum of psychosis is of course applicable to forensic patients, but there is something more in the atmosphere of the forensic locked ward than fear of "... the potential outbreak of actual violence that is the projected version of the intrapsychic violence" (Hinshelwood, 1987a, p. 210). Forensic patients have already acted violently, often with catastrophic outcomes: men, women and children have been assaulted, raped or killed. To paraphrase Hinshelwood, it would be more accurate to say that the factual violence is always felt to be not so much potential as imminent in work with patients who have already crossed the boundary between phantasy and reality. Furthermore, when the prevalence of dual diagnosis—psychosis and personality disorder—is recognized, the nature of the leading anxiety in forensic institutions must be distinguished from that which characterizes work in ordinary psychiatric hospitals. We believe that emotional contact with dual diagnosis creates a double-barrelled counter-dread in staff: psychic obliteration plus/via exposure to horrific psychopathic sadism in all its invasive, perverse, violent and sexual permutations. Our starting point in considering the role of a Forensic Psychotherapy Department is that staff in forensic settings unconsciously inhabit the emotional world of Oedipus Rex, and that the Oedipal situation in its most primitive, concrete form—portrayed by Seneca rather than Sophocles—represents the central forensic drama which intrudes into the professional work and can make it blind or "murderous" towards human relations between staff and patients and within the multidisciplinary teams:

> I saw things in the darkness moving many pale
> masks lifted and sinking I saw dark rivers and
> marshes I saw writhing things
>
> I could hear human voices and the screeching and
> laughing of mouths that were never on earth I heard
> sobbing deeper than anything on earth
>
> I saw every disease I knew their faces I heard them
> and knew their voices I saw every torment every

> injury every horror spinning like flames and shadows
> sickening forms faces mouths reaching up clutching
> towards us and crying
>
> I saw the plague of this city bloated blood
> oozing from every orifice grinning up on a
> sliding mountain of corpses [Hughes, 1969, p. 34]

In these verses Creon is describing his dawning awareness of the consequences of Oedipus' actions. He is like a member of staff who discovers the emotional essence of the task in forensic settings—encounter with madness and perversion enacted—and is terrified. The nature of forensic work is precisely the management of terror: terror of becoming the next victim of a patient's repeated index offence; terror of what one might feel like doing to prevent this; terror of what proximity to such extreme impulses and actions might ignite through emotional (seductive) contagion; terror of contact with the persecuting depression which may arise when insight looms; terror finally that, if as staff we "murder" lively interaction in order to survive our multiple terrors, we become psychologically like the patients: "murderers".

Countertransference

Countertransference is the staff member's basic relational potential. In psychoanalytic theory, it is the clinician's counter-response to the patient's approach (the transference). Etchegoyen, following Sandler et al. (1973), discerns that "counter" has two meanings, "opposed" and "parallel", "as in 'act and counteract', 'attack and counterattack' . . . [and] 'point and counterpoint' . . . These two meanings operate continuously and sometimes contradictorily in the definitions. When we speak of countertransference in the first sense, we mean that just as the analysand has his transference, so the analyst also has his. The countertransference is defined according to its direction—from here [analyst] to there [patient]—but it also establishes a balance, a counterpoint, which arises from the understanding that one's own reaction is not independent of what comes from the other" (Etchegoyen, 1991, p. 267). Since everyday experiences abundantly show us that "one's own reaction is not independent of what comes from the other", staff responses to patients (as individuals and as groups) are perhaps the most untapped and undervalued resource in the forensic setting. As we have mentioned, they are ignored because they are usually disturbing and even terrifying; and they remain neglected if no sustained organizational focus exists which could bring them to collective light and offer structures to contain and learn from them. This is where a Forensic Psychotherapy Department can make a contribution to the institution.

Much psychoanalytic research after about 1950, when Heimann (1950) and Racker (1968) almost simultaneously re-emphasized and elaborated Freud's (1912) allusion to the countertransference as a sensitive instrument which could detect emotional currents in the patient, has focused on the use of countertransference in the service of understanding the patient's fluctuating experience of the clinical interaction. Key contributions have been made by Bion (1961, 1984), Segal (1977, 1997), Ogden (1983), Pick (1985), Rosenfeld (1987), Joseph (1989) and Steiner (1993, 2006). These are technically sophisticated reflections on intensive clinical experience, and they pose a serious question for work in completely different settings: can the gap between the psychoanalytic consulting room and the forensic ward be bridged in a manner which acknowledges the differences and guards against the splitting dynamics adumbrated by Hinshelwood? Our experience is that a start can certainly be made in constructing some spans of this bridge, and we are convinced that countertransference is the central span from which to suspend interventions by a Forensic Psychotherapy Department. What is clear is that emotional responses to patients, whether directly or indirectly evoked, must be managed—contained (held in mind), sustained and carefully explored—in order to glean their significance. Two examples from forensic work will demonstrate the complexity and the promise of this process.

Too close for comfort

A young female nurse in training had been working for a considerable time on a secure rehabilitation ward for male patients. She was friendly and clearly popular, although she remained predominantly silent during the weekly ward Community Meeting of staff and patients. On one occasion, with fifteen patients and six staff present, the Ward Manager announced near the end of the meeting that Miss A, the young nurse, would be finishing her placement on the ward to return to college. This intervention in itself was unanticipated and refreshing, a product of over five years' work together between staff and a member of the Forensic Psychotherapy Department attached to the ward. Often on forensic wards patients and staff move suddenly; although some members of the ward are obviously in the know that a transfer has been requested by a member of staff or that a patient is due to move, usually no prior indication is given in the Community Meeting. Consequently, from the communal point of view, people come and go precipitously—almost as though they have died suddenly; and the ritual response, after the person has left and it becomes obvious in the meeting that X, who has probably been around for years, is gone, is: who is going to replace him/her? – that is if there is any response at all. Absence is intolerable in the forensic setting, both in prospect and in retrospect; the body must be replaced concretely and immediately or eradicated from memory.

The female nurse responded with evident embarrassment, looking shyly at the floor and shaking her head from side to side when several of the patients in unison, hearing the Ward Manager's comments, surprisingly suggested a goodbye meal. The Psychotherapist could sense their affection towards her and the feeling of dejection which soon replaced it as the futility of their proposal sank in. The Ward Manager quickly thanked the nurse and clarified that she did not want her leaving to be marked by any formal occasion. The Community Meeting ended, and staff proceeded to the after-group session for reflection on our experiences of the meeting.

Miss A carried her embarrassment into the meeting, where colleagues sympathized with her plight, and after some brief teasing regarding her shyness, they all seemed inclined to omit the issue from further discussion. The topic then shifted to a serious incident between a patient and another female nurse. This had occurred the previous night and had only been alluded to vaguely in the Community Meeting when some remarks had been made about poor lighting in the long corridor near the patients' rooms. From these comments no one could have known that a patient had been sitting on a sofa near the end of the corridor and had exposed himself to the nurse while she was checking on the patients. The dangerousness of this patient, particularly his "psychopathic cleverness" in being able to deny his intimidating impact, had become the main topic of our group and threatened to pull it away from its brief to discuss the Community Meeting, rather as the patient had intruded himself into the nurse's rounds.

The Psychotherapist said that Miss A had felt in a very difficult position and obviously had not wanted the patients or staff to celebrate their work together. She looked up and smiled. He added that the patients' affection had seemed genuine, so that the nurse's reticence, however understandable, was sad. The Psychotherapist could not know in advance whether from the nurse's perspective his words would feel like being on the receiving end of a repeated, humiliating exposure or be received as thoughts about the work. Another nurse remarked that patients could feel rejected. She went on to say that the two themes which had come up in our after-group might be connected: patients whom staff considered highly threatening perverts might feel that the failure to take up their positive overtures was a punishment. If so, patients would feel dirty and useless. Later that day, in the weekly Reflective Practice group for nurses, a third nurse who had been present in the earlier meetings spoke at length about her experiences when she was in another patient's room. He had told her that putting a cigarette butt or banana skin in his bin gave him a sexual sensation, but he was very uncertain whether it was homosexual or heterosexual. This patient is a very confused, paranoid man who, without frightening his nurse (who had nonetheless been exceedingly uncomfortable), seemed to be making a rare contact in telling her about the state of his mind and his bewilderment over relationships.

Postscript

In the very next Community Meeting, with a new patient and visiting staff in attendance, we went through our usual introductions. Each person in turn, moving around the circle of chairs, would give his or her name, invariably first names only with the addition of the word "patient" or "staff". When the turn of a male nurse came, he said, "M, patient". A tsunami shock wave swept across the room as the emotional expressions flowed across the nurse's face. A smile of total mortification quickly gave way to a rictus of utter horror which in turn evolved into a wave of "taking the piss" laughter from staff which seemed to submerge the whole experience. An identification between "staff" and "patient", emerging from the unconscious, had subverted a necessary (defensive) conviction regarding the essential and apparently irrefutable distinction between them.

We think it is extremely significant that this particular nurse had participated in the previous Community Meeting and was present in the after-group discussion. The patients' affection for the departing female nurse had evidently touched a responsive chord in staff, a counterpart wish to respond affectionately ("point and counterpoint") which momentarily decreased the predominant countertransference of "act and counteract", "attack and counterattack" to defend against sexual abuse. The conflicting responses need to be remembered and worked on by the whole staff group, for no individual alone is strong enough or even in a position to know how colleagues may be affected. It is also all too easy to leave the most disturbing emotional responses and conflicting experiences with junior members of the team, whose discomfiture (as with the female nurse) can, without careful group vigilance, be subjected to teasing and evasion. Thus a concealed version of the sadistically controlling abuse is enacted within the staff. As this example shows, however, group care for the individual staff member's emotional responses may itself be experienced as humiliating and abusive attention; this was the Psychotherapist's countertransference in the group while he considered his comments to Miss A, but his long working relationship with the team allowed him to take the risk. Care is always susceptible to being perverted in the forensic context, and so it is understandably avoided. The next example shows how communication about countertransference threatens to become a persecution which must be worked with to gain further understanding of a patient's profoundly painful state of mind.

"I want to bring up a communication problem"

Arriving somewhat late to the Community Meeting, which she had been attending regularly over the last few months, the rather aristocratic and fiery Spanish Consultant Psychiatrist said she needed to bring a communication problem to our attention regarding a middle-aged Latin American patient for whom she was responsible. She seemed uncharacteristically tense, and abruptly explained that a very serious lapse had occurred regarding the patient's leave the previous weekend. This was an extremely important occasion for the patient; Home Office permission had been sought and granted some time before, but the patient had not been escorted by nursing staff. The Consultant paused briefly and then added quickly that although she had put an enormous amount of work into the matter, she had forgotten to sign a specific form. She apologized softly, but went on to claim that nursing staff had known about the leave and had been aware of its significance to the patient. Nurses should have provided an escort, she had heard that few were around at the time and they were negligent.

The Psychotherapist realized that having skirted over her own mistake, the Consultant had launched a critical investigation into the nurses; he tried to clarify for himself and for the others present at the meeting the nature of the unsigned form. It turned out to be vitally important. The Consultant was silent. The Nurse Manager was in no mood for discussion; nor did he intend to ignore the Consultant's tone. He pointed out firmly that (1) they had been fully aware of the planned leave; (2) there had been ample staff on duty, prepared to do the escort; and (3) the Consultant had failed to sign the crucial form authorizing leave, so that the nurses on duty that day could not go ahead. He became increasingly fierce towards the Consultant for attacking his staff in this public manner. The patient involved looked relaxed and did not express any particular concern: yes, he had planned to go but he had arranged to take leave next weekend.

The mood was extremely tense as staff convened for the after-group. The Consultant pressed her point that this patient had been badly let down by the nurses. The Nurse Manager reiterated that the essential leave form, entirely the responsibility of the Consultant (or, in her absence, her junior), had not been completed. Nurses could be exposed to charges of professional dereliction of duty, with severe consequences, had they permitted a patient to leave the hospital without authorization by the Responsible Medical Officer. His nursing colleagues nodded furiously. Out of ignorance, the Psychotherapist asked where the patient had intended to go. The Consultant replied that it had been the anniversary of his mother's death, and a service with the family had taken place. Now the patient had missed a unique event; the unspoken implication was that the situation was irreparable. For some reason the Psychotherapist wondered why the patient was in a forensic unit. "He killed his mother," said the Consultant.

Again—and this is absolutely characteristic of forensic work—we found ourselves in the world of Greek tragedy: an Oresteian variant of the (negative) Oedipal configuration.

Clytemnestra

> Orestes, my child! Don't point at me with your sword.
> See these breasts that fed you when you were helpless.
> These were your first pillows when you were helpless.

Orestes

> Pylades, can a man kill his mother?
> Can he perform anything more dreadful
> Than the murder of his own mother?
> What shall I do? [Hughes, 1999, p. 133]

Amazement and pain give way to incoherent dread. What language might be used to grasp what had struck us? The Psychotherapist acknowledged how much work the Consultant had devoted to facilitate this patient's leave and was puzzled by the unsigned form. She could not shed much light on this glaring lapse, and the Psychotherapist wondered if the patient had struggled with divided feelings about such an event. The Consultant stated flatly that the patient had wanted to go, the whole family wanted him to be there, and it had been carefully planned; but in the current atmosphere she was clearly reluctant to engage in further discussion about her mistake. She indicated her feeling that the very thought that there might be something worth exploring was absurd; further, the Psychotherapist was becoming a nuisance. Until that moment, they had worked well together on the ward.

Heimann summarizes her view on countertransference in an astonishing formulation: "From the point of view I am stressing, the analyst's countertransference is not only part and parcel of the analytic relationship, but it is the patient's *creation*, it is a part of the patient's personality" (1950, p. 83). The Consultant's emotional responses to her patient in the specific circumstances described above are her own feelings and thoughts and reactions. But work with patients who are often profoundly dissociated from their feelings, impulses and effects on others creates a clinical milieu in which Heimann's proposition is entirely plausible *if subjected to the mandatory caution she emphasizes*: countertransference responses must be both sustained and subordinated to disciplined investigation before potential clues to the patient's state of mind can emerge.

Subsequent exploration brought to light how peculiarly this patient had been behaving in the weeks preceding the leave. From a rather pleasant, open and articulate stance he began to attract the attention of nursing staff by delinquent behaviour. He was frequently seen whispering in small groups of known drug takers. He lied about a "herb" which he told the Ward Manager he mixed with his tobacco—it turned out to be marijuana. He contended (implausibly, in the Ward Manager's estimation) at a ward round, in his Consultant's presence, that he had been forced by two other patients to bring them drugs; and when he burst into tears, murmuring some words in Spanish, his Consultant believed him: a veteran of a high-secure hospital who never acted like he could be pushed around. Finally, he lied again to staff by claiming that he had not been reimbursed with a small amount of his money which he had asked a nursing assistant to take in order to buy something for him. The nursing assistant had not been able to make the purchase and had refunded the money, but the patient nevertheless told the Ward Manager that he had not been given his money and was given the amount by the Manager. Yet in a subsequent Community Meeting attended by the Service Director, the patient complained about the untrustworthiness of staff who tell lies, and was advised by the Director that he could make an official complaint for theft. The hapless nursing assistant was incredulous when these developments were discussed in a Reflective Practice group, and poignantly stated repeatedly that he had indeed returned the patient's money in front of two witnesses.

We were witnessing in this episode a continual torrent of blame and complementary assertions of innocence reverberating throughout the ward from meeting to meeting, contaminating relationships within the staff team and invading their creative work. Lies, guilt and "communication problems" within individuals' minds resonated disastrously within their groups. Responsibility could not be faced when the "index offence" was irreparable. The Consultant, identified with one aspect of her patient, had glossed over her "index offence" and attributed guilt to others. In turn they denied their culpability and went on the offensive. "Staff" had *become* "patient", not (as in our first example) on the basis of resonating, if terrifying, affection, but in identification with the remorselessly warring parts of the patient's severed personality. He sat bemused initially, the wronged party; but he eventually relished the barrister's brief in the High Court of the Community Meeting presided over by the Service Director, having decimated the link between Consultant and nurses.

Chorus

> Can the poor, scorched brains of Orestes
> Figure out all the factors? Can he solve
> The arithmetic of the unfinished
> That shunts this curse from one generation to the next?
> Who can bring it to an end?
> When can it be brought to an end?
> How can it be brought to an end? [Hughes, 1999, p. 143]

We have described the nature of anxiety in forensic settings and put forward the concept of countertransference as the fulcrum for interventions by a Forensic Psychotherapy Department. Orestes—the patient—cannot "solve the arithmetic of the unfinished"; nor can the multidisciplinary team or the Consultant Forensic Psychotherapist. The issue is more whether the "shunt[ing of] this curse from one generation to the next", from the recurrent echoes in the mind of the patient to one professional staff group after another throughout the organization, can be contained rather than continuously acted out to the detriment of both patient and staff. It is the mindless repetition of "all the factors" which must be diminished.

In the preceding chapters, the contributors have described a diversified range of interventions deployed by a Psychotherapy Department within a Forensic Service which can contribute substantially to the process of containing the "scorched brains" of everyone. Based on the premise that forensic patients are unable to face the magnitude of their anxiety and guilt and that they consequently "empty" their personalities into the milieu in the most disturbing ways, the focus of a psychotherapeutic contribution must be on the minds of the people-in-their structures (groups) which comprise that milieu and cannot be confined to assessing and treating individual patients. We conceptualize our interventions as windows on the social countertransference system, the multiple, scattered arrays of interpersonal impacts which patients have on staff. A window is both a frame and a view. Each of the interventions offers a container for different aspects of the countertransference, and the combination of linked interventions provides an opportunity for integration.

At the hub of the ward milieu is the Community Meeting. There is a substantial literature on large group dynamics in general and on the function of the Community Meeting in particular, primarily in the context of ward and hospital settings organized along Therapeutic Community lines (Kreeger, 1975; Gordon & Whiteley, 1979; Hinshelwood, 1987b). The intense anxieties and splitting mechanisms prevailing in the large group make it an exceedingly difficult emotional experience. However, in no other arena is it possible for staff to come so close to knowing what mental illness feels like, to gradually become aware of how they attempt to shield themselves from this experience and—especially in forensic settings—to glimpse how violent, psychologically if not physically, their responses to "threats to identity" (Turquet, 1975; Main, 1975) can be. Insofar as the large group dynamics mirror those in the even larger group/organization within which staff work, the Community Meeting provides a setting in which staff can identify processes and pressures which "invisibly" affect them every day as members of an institution.

When all the patients and staff meet together regularly, it is possible to struggle to relate to one another in order to transact the "business" of the ward community (hygiene, food, repairs, activities); to further the clinical task of patient evaluation in a challenging social setting, including risk assessment; and (most fundamentally) to monitor the interactions between the patient and staff sub-groupings collectively represented in the meeting (Hinshelwood, 1979). Present as individuals and as sub-group, staff are available much as Pirandello's characters in search of an author, and there is no lack of potential authors/patients in the Community Meeting. From our perspective, what is vital is to characterize the predominant countertransference responses of staff as individuals and as members of a group—to the Meeting (the phantasy of the group as an object), to individual patients, and to the patients as a sub-group. This is the task of the psychotherapist, who attends the Community Meeting and facilitates an after-group in which staff can discuss their participation, experience and reactions (which in turn can be linked to understanding the current states of mind of specific patients or of the patients as a group), as well as identify possible blind spots, impulses to retaliate, inclinations to withdraw and incipient divisions in the multidisciplinary team.

Reflective Practice has been described from several angles. We hold groups for distinct professions (nurses, occupational therapists, psychiatrists, social workers) and groups open to all members of the multidisciplinary team on the ward. We also offer reflective practice to managers. It has been widely accepted that reflective practice is an essential component of good clinical work. In forensic settings, this input tends to be valued in word and resisted in fact, for discussing one's work and relationships with colleagues in a group threatens to disclose the enormous difficulties, uncertainties and fears experienced by individuals, to reveal serious interpersonal strains within the team, or to demonstrate the anti-task, defensive motivations of the staff group as a whole.

We assume that it is at least as difficult for forensic patients to face, learn from and regret their catastrophic actions as it would be for anyone. Deep depression and suicidal states are often precipitated by dawning awareness of consequences; the response is to cut off, and we are confronted with the severing of insight and reflection which is the most common presenting symptom of psychosis. Patients fear any awareness of their experiences as perpetrators or victims, but staff members, who must remain aware in order to work with their patients, soon find that even the most tactful attempts to "remind" patients of their offences are extremely unwelcome. At the extreme, staff are perceived as persecutors and jailers of "innocent victims". The more patients empty their minds of painful memories, the more staff members' minds and case notes are filled by them. Ultimately, the combined burden of remembering and the unrelenting pressure from patients to forget affects staff members and teams. The fragmenting, dissociative tendencies within the patients' minds reverberate within the multidisciplinary team and the organization. Nevertheless, precisely because forensic patients do not just lack an ability to reflect but splinter and destroy their capacity to do so, for long periods of time the deficit in patients' capacity to reflect must be compensated by an amplification of that capacity in staff.

Patients are treated by professionals with very different skills who offer a wide range of interventions. It is essential for members of the multidisciplinary team to meet together sufficiently frequently to clarify how their varied interventions may or may not add up to a coherent treatment approach. The effects of the centrifugal forces just mentioned make this far from a foregone conclusion. Patients also respond very differently to individual staff, distinct professional groups, diverse treatment interventions, and to the differential status of occupants of managerial roles. Each member of the team may have, as a result of patients' impacts, radically conflicting perceptions of and feelings towards particular patients, and may make incompatible recommendations for treatment. Or the best planned treatment approach may be dismantled, to the puzzlement of clinicians, who in consequence feel incompetent or guilty.

Pastoral support and individual supervision of staff have their place but do not define their tasks as integrating the elements of severe patient psychopathology ("lack of insight" converted into calamitous action); intensely emotional, frightening and fragmenting impacts on individuals and staff teams; and fundamental but problematic organizational imperatives to harmonize treatment and security. Nor do they ensure the coherence of overall staff interventions. Rather than a supportive group for the staff, reflective practice is a crucial clinical tool to support the primary task of staff: mindful engagement with patients.

Reflective practice groups for multidisciplinary staff teams, separate professional groups and managers, facilitated by consultants trained in psychodynamics, group dynamics and organizational (systemic) processes, are the *sine qua non* of this integration within the forensic service. Through sustained participation at the level of service policy making, including active involvement in clinical governance, we have succeeded in making both Community Meetings and Reflective Practice mandatory elements of the treatment programme. Members of the Forensic Psychotherapy Department, no exception to this rule, meet weekly to discuss their own work, and consider occasional external consultation (by video link) extremely useful as a second layer check on their countertransference immersion as members of the organization. As with all other staff groups, psychotherapists need regular, structured opportunities to recover their professional identity.

Training initiatives from a Forensic Psychotherapy Department must guard against the assumption, mentioned by Hinshelwood (1987a), that multidisciplinary staff are learning to be psychotherapists. We have developed a Certificate/Diploma in Individual, Group and Organizational Dynamics in Work with the Severely Mentally Ill in Acute and Forensic Settings in conjunction with a highly respected academic institution. The course includes academic seminars; an application group in which students discuss their clinical work in role to examine how the theoretical concepts illuminate (or not) their own professional, individual and group interactions with patients; an experiential group (similar in size to ward Community Meetings); and an intensive Group Relations Event based on the Tavistock/A.K. Rice model. The objectives of this training are to enable staff to identify and understand the unconscious pressures on their functioning in role arising from dyadic, small group and multiple group/large group (institutional) transference-countertransference dynamics. The training is strongly supported at executive level within the Trust, and staff are recruited specifically in order to be better able to participate in Community Meetings, to use Reflective Practice, and to contribute to the therapeutic milieu: graduates will be the clinical managers of the future.

Assessments and psychotherapy in individual, group and systemic family modalities are nuclear components of a Forensic Psychotherapy Department as a specialized clinical entity and as a training ground for junior doctors, psychiatrists in psychotherapy and other professionals. Experienced psychotherapists need to have close contact with patients in order to keep in touch with the extremely complex, sensitive and taxing transference-countertransference conundrums posed by this work. Trainees in forensic psychotherapy, group analysis and family therapy, through supervised assessments and treatment, learn to contain the inevitable turmoil.

Assessments are immensely valuable when discussed together with the multidisciplinary team. The objective is to combine a psychodynamic understanding of a patient's personality, repertoire of core self-object (other) relational scenarios and offending behaviours with colleagues' evaluations of and involvements with that patient on the ward. Above all, in accordance with the fundamental task of a Forensic Service, joint discussions contribute to the assessment and management of risk through the elucidation of interactions with the patient which reveal derivatives, in action or evoked emotional responses, of the index offence. Of special significance in this respect is to become aware of anxieties which may impel staff to ignore their awareness of such derivatives.

A basic problem in sharing assessment and treatment consultations is to establish both an appropriate mode for handling communications and a means of communication. Participation in ward rounds, Care Plan Approach meetings and other multidisciplinary forums precludes, for example, a psychotherapist concealing that his patient has just revealed in a session that he had been sexually abused or had committed an unrecorded assault. Ward staff need to be alert to possible effects of the patient's disclosure on his state of mind or actions after the session. But care must be taken within the meeting to clarify the boundaries of confidentiality concerning the new information. In particular, those members of the team who in specified circumstances may refer explicitly to it in subsequent contacts with the patient must be clearly differentiated from those who need to keep it in mind.

By a means of communication we imply the elaboration of a basic language, founded on an interpersonal dynamic dimension, which can serve as a common currency within the multidisciplinary team for the exchange and comparison of experiences with forensic patients. The development of this language is a vital contribution of a Forensic Psychotherapy Department. Our natural professional language is rooted in psychoanalysis. We talk to each other about transference, countertransference, projective identification and containment. For example, we might describe the projective identification of murderous superego aspects into the staff, whose custodial, monitoring functions are then experienced as punitive control to which patients both submit and retaliate; damage, loss and guilt are thus erased from the patient's inner experience, and sado-masochistic scenarios are enacted between patient and staff which, however painful and frightening, are more tolerable than the potentially suicidal persecution which looms from within as the patient becomes more aware. However, for us the meanings of these concepts do not arise just from a theoretical tradition but also from personal experiences as patients while training. While our specific language grounds the interventions of a Forensic Psychotherapy Department, we have sought to fashion a more usable and understandable language which captures the interpersonal dynamic dimension of everyday life.

Many protocols for formulating the interpersonal dynamic dimension in terms of attachment or relationship patterns are available for the clinical assessment of patients and for research. In line with our psychoanalytic orientation and long clinical experience with personality disorders, we have always found Kernberg's emphasis on "activated relational dyads" (Koenigsberg et al, 2000, p. 16) useful in assessments (Kernberg, 1984), treatment and, more broadly, as a framework for an intuitively meaningful and dramatic language of self and other relating under the aegis of specific emotions which colour the interpersonal interaction and mutual perceptions of the actors. A recent publication by a consortium of psychoanalytic organizations, the *Psychodynamic Diagnostic Manual* (PDM) (2006) is an immensely fruitful expansion of Kernberg's focus on the delineation of disordered personality patterns and their effects on interpersonal relations. Drawing on advances in neuroscience, outcome studies and empirical research into the complexities of healthy and pathological patterns of emotional, cognitive and personality functioning—all of which increasingly demonstrate the rapidly diminishing scientific returns of the DSM's ever more discrete, excessively delimited and therefore oversimplified descriptions of observable symptoms—psychodynamic diagnosis instead locates the functioning of each patient within an in-depth nexus of relationships. The patient's capacities for "affect tolerance, regulation and expression; coping strategies and defenses; [. . .] understanding self and others; and quality of relationships" (PDM Task Force, 2006, p. 3) are assessed and meticulously interlinked. In the context of our concern with clinical communication within multidisciplinary teams, the project overall could be characterized, in terms used by two of its contributors, as a search for "a standard vocabulary for case description [based on] psychodynamics without jargon" (Shedler & Westen, 2006, pp. 579–581).

Operationalized Psychodynamic Diagnostics (OPD) is a further contribution in this area (OPD Task Force, 2001). OPD is a complex, comprehensive, manualized assessment tool which combines descriptive phenomenological diagnostics (ICD-10, DSM-IV) with psychodynamic features derived from psychoanalysis. Patients are assessed on five axes: (I) experience of illness and prerequisites for treatment (expectations and motivation); (II) relation (transference and countertransference); (III) conflict (internal interacting with external); (IV) structure (capacities and deficiencies of mental structure, for example, self-observation and control, affect regulation); and (V) mental and psychosomatic disorders (psychopathological phenomena according to established psychiatric classifications).

From our perspective, Axis II, which elicits the predominant transference-countertransference configurations, is particularly relevant. The basic procedure is to conceptualize aspects of the patient's core relationship patterns by (1) clarifying how the patient characteristically experiences himself and the other in interaction with himself, and (2) describing how the other (staff member) usually experiences the patient as well as him/herself in their interactions. From this material it is possible to hypothesize the significant internalized object relationships of the patient and the manner in which they may influence external relationships on the ward. Most importantly, the consultant and the multidisciplinary team meeting in Reflective Practice or in other clinical/managerial groups are provided with a medium through which they can validate the meaningfulness of their emotional responses, compare and explore them with colleagues, and develop a cross-disciplinary language which, whatever particular professionals' distinctive tasks, allows communication about interpersonal relationships with patients to be a shared focus of clinical work.

In conjunction with a structured risk assessment/management tool such as the HCR-20 (Webster et al, 1997), which avoids the limitations of actuarial prediction by recommending the elaboration for each patient of potential interpersonal scenarios at differing levels of risk, the use of the interpersonal dynamic dimension as a common language turns life on the ward into a crucial matrix for the generation and careful evaluation of actual scenarios as they are lived by patients and staff. This language represents the dual focus of a Forensic Psychotherapy Department: to integrate its own clinical work with the endeavours of colleagues from other professions in the service and to defend the principle of integration of all the work, whether bio-, psycho- or social, within the overall clinical setting.

In our view, there is an *essential prerequisite* for all of the interventions described in this book: being with the patients; being with the staff; being seen to be with the patients by the staff. Members of a Forensic Psychotherapy Department must suffer the impacts of patients in the presence of staff who witness these impacts. This is not in order to model for colleagues how to be with the patient (although of course we learn from one another), for any such claim to be an exemplar would be all too liable to the organizational splitting (denigration/idealization) Hinshelwood (1987a) discerns. Rather it is to ally oneself with colleagues who, especially in the case of psychiatric nurses, must endure emotional contact with forensic patients for far longer than the psychotherapist. By putting in the time, usually years, and particularly in that most threatening forum, the ward Community Meeting, psychotherapists can gradually earn their other interventions, which accordingly have greater chances of being received. We are proposing that the integration of psychoanalytic work into the Forensic Service depends fundamentally on an integration in the mind on the part of members of a Forensic Psychotherapy Department: keeping in mind "the other 23 hours" (Stanton & Schwartz, 1954, p. 9) of the patients' and the staff's fraught lives together. And this integration is embodied in a real presence in those lives on the ward and at all levels of the hospital structure.

Bion, in his seminal study of countertransference in groups, refers to the crucial ability to realize when "[the analyst] feels he is being manipulated so as to be playing a part, no matter how difficult to recognize, in somebody else's phantasy . . ." (1961, p. 149). Carpy (1989) has highlighted the importance in psychoanalytic work of the patient's observations of the analyst's efforts to tolerate the strains imposed by the patient. The patient watches the analyst struggling with difficulties, and the analyst's capacity to bear that challenge—or not—affects the course of the treatment. Britton (1989, 1998) discusses the origins of the reflective capacity inherent in these contributions, which he considers in terms of subjectivity, objectivity and triangular space: "If the link between the parents perceived in love and hate can be tolerated in the child's mind, it provides the child with a prototype for an object relationship of a third kind in which he or she is a witness and not a participant. A *third position* then comes into existence from which object relationships can be observed. Given this, we can also envisage being observed. This provides us with a capacity for seeing ourselves in interaction with others and for entertaining another point of view while retaining our own—for observing ourselves while being ourselves" (Britton, 1998, p. 41–42).

These psychoanalytic expressions of the fundamental importance of being able to witness without intruding orient the interventions of a Forensic Psychotherapy Department. Through our reliable, long-term presence on the ward, staff observe us absorbing and contending with the psychic assaults of patients as we witness staff engaging with and evading—we are all frightened clinicians—the terrible dilemmas posed by close contact with forensic patients. For of all the patients encountered in mental health services, these are the least likely to be able to adopt a reflective stance in relation to the turbulence in their own minds and in relation to other people: Oedipus intruded catastrophically into the lives of both his parents, as well as into his organs of observation.

As individuals, members of multiple small groups and participants in the large group processes of our mental health organizations (Hinshelwood & Skogstad, 2000; Hinshelwood & Chiesa, 2001; Armstrong, 2005), professionals are constantly subjected to and participate in the emotional bombardments of "toxic nourishment" (Eigen, 1999) which especially characterize that most toxic of "toxic institutions" (Campling, Davies & Farquharson, 2004), the forensic setting. The countertransference represents our experiential, responsive contribution to relationships as well as our self-blindings. We adopt and enact our "required" countertransferences at individual, group and organizational levels—in counterpoint with the patients' transferences (Ezriel, 1959)—to protect us from more alarming insights into our "avoided" countertransferences and their expected "calamitous" outcomes. But this is why the alliance of a Forensic Psychotherapy Department with colleagues must attempt to offset the prevailing destruction of the sense of perception by struggling together to work through the layers of countertransference in order to get in touch with the almost insoluble mental states of forensic patients and to reduce or modify their reiteration within the service.

In forensic settings, the countertransference is the most frightening, ignored and valuable untapped resource of staff teams. The interventions of a Forensic Psychotherapy Department, focused on a psychoanalytic understanding of the transference-countertransference, are far from a panacea; but they do constitute both a full participation in the countertransference and an indispensable collaborative effort to reconstruct the capacity to acknowledge, observe and explore it.

AFTERWORD

David Armstrong

The contributions brought together in this seminal book invite a bifocal reading or attention. From one perspective, as the title indicates, they offer an inside description of the "emotional storm" created out of the encounter with a particular population of disturbed and disturbing, damaged and damaging patients (Bion, 1979). What makes this storm so difficult both to bear and to understand is the obliteration of emotional meaning at the heart of the patients' experience and by extension of one's own experience of that experience; and its substitution by what Anne Aiyegbusi and Gillian Tuck refer to as "communication by impact" (Chapter 1).

The vignettes of experience that thread throughout the book illustrate in painful detail how both the storm and its substitution affect and infect relations and interactions at every level of the containing institution: between not only patients and staff, but patients and patients, staff and staff, staff and management, management and stakeholders. One might think of this as a process of emotional or psychological contagion, in which the underlying dynamics of disorder and the defences mobilised against disorder ripple throughout the whole system.

For the reader, like myself, familiar with this world only from a relatively safe position—occasional consultant, visitor, researcher, concerned outsider—these experiences lived from the inside are hard to witness, even at the distance of one's desk. They are not, however, the whole story, and this links to the second perspective from which, taken together, the different contributions can be read.

In one sense the title of the book might be said to be misleading, suggesting that what is offered is simply a description of a particular emotional world, viewed through the lens of an extended reading of countertransference phenomena in forensic settings. But what marks the book's importance, in my view, for the understanding and practice of work in these settings is not so much what is described as the use to which this may be put, i.e. the significance and function of countertransference as a therapeutic vehicle, not just for disclosing meaning but for modulating action, decision, policy and response at every level, clinical and managerial.

The idea that countertransference, "conceived as a link between the patient and the responsive mind and sensibilities of the staff" (Introduction), can furnish a basis for "ongoing concerned enquiry" is not in itself new. However, what gives the contributors' use of this idea a more distinctive slant is firstly its extension across the whole social field that furnishes the "milieu" in which patients live and interact with each other and with staff.

From this viewpoint, implicit in many of the descriptive vignettes throughout the book, no single interaction or encounter is likely to capture what might be termed the full emotional undertone of the patients' enactments. Rather, in a striking image used by the editors in their concluding chapter, each interaction or encounter is viewed as just one "window on the social countertransference system, the multiple scattered arrays of interpersonal impacts which patients have on staff . . . (offering) a container for different aspects of the countertransference" (Conclusion).

The implications of this position are far-reaching indeed, since what is implied, as the editors go on to remark, is that the work of understanding, of giving meaning to what is happening and hence of modulating response, turns on an ability and readiness to bring together, reflect on and work through the fragments or facets of experience held by different actors in different spaces and at different times. It is perhaps in this sense that one may understand Stanley

Ruszczynski's argument that for those patients "whose disturbance and dangerousness as expressed through their criminal, perverse or violent actions are a central factor . . . the institution as a whole offers the most significant possibility for treatment and is in essence the primary therapeutic agent" (Chapter Five).

This argument, implicit not so much in each contribution as in their combined impact, might be taken as offering a new perspective on the concept of a therapeutic community, interpreted less as the expression of a particular therapeutic ideology than as the acknowledgement of a pervasive therapeutic reality arising out of the nature of the work, with these patients and in these settings, and its distributed emotional undertone.

Such a position raises the question of how this acknowledgement can be realised in practice: that is, not simply recognised in the abstract but brought to inform the patterning of reflection, communication and interaction across and between the disciplines, teams and functions that make up the containing institution and within each of which emotional experience may serve as one "window of meaning". Gabriel Kirtchuk, David Reiss and John Gordon's discussion of new approaches to clinical communication (Chapter Six) and the editors' concluding discussion of the varieties of reflective practice implemented in their own service, in particular, go a fair way in addressing this question.

In his Foreword to the book, Robert Hinshelwood refers to "the possibility that there are limits to containing", that patients or some patients may not be interested in or able to make use of the disclosure of meaning, a dynamic that can be reinforced by the "enforced helplessness" associated with the realities of institutional confinement. (One might speculate that if so, this dynamic is likely to be mirrored in the staff's own countertransferential experiences.) In fact, this resistant undercurrent is evident and acknowledged throughout many of these contributions (cf. in particular Carine Minne's account of "The Dreaded and Dreading Patient and Therapist" in Chapter Two).

However, one way of reading this book is that it maps out both an approach and a determination to test the extent and significance of these limits in practice, without seeking to predetermine the outcome. In this respect it may stand as an unusually bold and uncompromising example of psychodynamically informed action research and the contribution this can offer, drawing on the intelligence afforded by emotional experience, to the restoring of both meaning and agency. Viewed in this way, the book both speaks to and has a relevance for practitioners, managers and consultants well beyond the boundaries of any single enterprise.

REFERENCES

Adshead, G. (1998). Psychiatric Staff as Attachment Figures. *British Journal of Psychiatry 172*: 64–69.

Adshead, G. (2004). Three Degrees of Security: Attachment and Forensic Institutions. In: F. Pfäfflin, & G. Adshead (Eds.), *A Matter of Security: The Application of Attachment Theory to Forensic Psychiatry and Psychotherapy* (pp. 147–166). London: Jessica Kingsley.

Armstrong, D. (2005). *Organization in the Mind: Psychoanalysis, Group Relations and Organizational Consultancy*. London: Karnac.

Benjamin, L.S. (1996). *Interpersonal Diagnosis and Treatment of Personality Disorders*. New York: Guilford Press.

Bion, W.R. (1957). Differentiation of the Psychotic from the Non-Psychotic Personalities. *Int. J. Psycho-Anal. 38*: 266–275.

Bion, W.R. (1958). On Arrogance. *Int. J. Psycho-Anal. 39*: 341–349.

Bion, W.R. (1959). Attacks on Linking. *Int. J. Psycho-Anal. 40*: 308–315.

Bion, W.R. (1961). *Experiences in Groups*. London: Tavistock.

Bion, W.R. (1962). A Theory of Thinking. Reprinted in: *Second Thoughts: Selected Papers on Psychoanalysis*. London: Karnac, 1984.

Bion, W.R. (1970). *Attention and Interpretation*. London: Tavistock.

Bion, W.R. (1976). Interview by Anthony G. Banet, Jr. Reprinted in: *The Tavistock Seminars*. London: Karnac, 2005.

Bion, W.R. (1979). Making the Best of a Bad Job. In: *Clinical Seminars and Four Papers*. Abingdon: Fleetwood Press, 1987.

Bion, W.R. (1984). *Second Thoughts: Selected Papers on Psychoanalysis*. London: Karnac.

Bion, W.R. (1992). *Cogitations*. London: Karnac.

Blackburn, R. (1998). Criminality and the Interpersonal Circle in Forensic Psychiatric Patients. *Criminal Justice and Behaviour 25*: 155–176.

Britton, R. (1989). The Missing Link: Parental Sexuality in the Oedipus Complex. In: R. Britton, M. Feldman and E. O'Shaugnessy (Eds.), *The Oedipus Complex Today: Clinical Implications*. London: Karnac.

Britton, R. (1998). *Belief and Imagination: Explorations in Psychoanalysis*. London: Routledge.

Britton, R. (2003). *Sex, Death, and the Superego: Experiences in Psychoanalysis*. London: Karnac.

Campling, P., Davies, S. & Farquharson, G. (Eds.) (2004). *From Toxic Institutions to Therapeutic Environments: Residential Settings in Mental Health Services*. London: Gaskell.

Carpy, D. Tolerating the Countertransference: a Mutative Process. *Int. J. Psycho-Anal. 70*: 287–294.

Cartwright, D. (2002). *Psychoanalysis, Violence and Rage-Type Murder*. Hove: Brunner Routledge.

Casement, P. (1985). *On Learning from the Patient*. London: Brunner-Routledge.

Chasseguet-Smirgel, J. (1984). *Creativity and Perversion*. New York: Norton.

Cordess, C. & Cox, M. (Eds.) (1996). *Forensic Psychotherapy: Crime, Psychodynamics and the Offender Patient*. London: Jessica Kingsley.

Cox, M. (1978). *Coding the Therapeutic Process: Problems of Encounter*. Oxford: Pergamon Press.

Cox, M. (1996). Psychodynamics and the Special Hospital: Road Blocks and Thought Blocks. In: C. Cordess & M. Cox (Eds.), *Forensic Psychotherapy: Crime, Psychodynamics and the Offender Patient, Vol. II: Mainly Practice* (pp. 433–448). London: Jessica Kingsley.

Cox, M. (1996). A Supervisor's View. In: C. Cordess & M. Cox (Eds.), *Forensic Psychotherapy: Crime, Psychodynamics and the Offender Patient, Vol. II: Mainly Practice* (pp. 199–223). London: Jessica Kingsley.

CSIP/NIMHE, CWP & Royal College of Psychiatrists (2005). *New Ways of Working for Psychiatrists: Enhancing Effective, Person-Centred Services through New Ways of Working in Multidisciplinary and Multi-Agency Contexts*. London: Department of Health.

Davies, R. (1996). The Inter-Disciplinary Network and the Internal World of the Offender. In: C. Cordess & M. Cox (Eds.), *Forensic Psychotherapy: Crime, Psychodynamics and the Offender Patient, Vol. II: Mainly Practice* (pp. 133–144). London: Jessica Kingsley.

De Zulueta, F. (1993). *From Pain to Violence: The Traumatic Roots of Destructiveness*. London: Whurr.

Doctor, R. (Ed.) (2003). *Dangerous Patients: A Psychodynamic Approach to Risk Assessment and Management*. London: Karnac.

Eigen, M. (1985). Towards Bion's Starting Point: Between Catastrophe and Death. *Int. J. Psycho-Anal. 66*: 321–330.

Eigen, M. (1999). *Toxic Nourishment*. London: Karnac.

Etchegoyen, R.H. (1991). *The Fundamentals of Psychoanalytic Technique*. London: Karnac.

Ezriel, H. (1959). Role of transference in psychoanalysis and other approaches to group treatment. *Acta Psychotherapeutica 7 (Suppl.)*: 101–116.

Fonagy, P., Gersely, G., Jurist, L. & Target, M. (2002). *Affect Regulation, Mentalization and the Development of the Self*. New York: Other Press.

Freud, A. (1946). *The Ego and the Mechanisms of Defense*. New York: International Universities Press.

Freud, S. (1910). The Future Prospects of Psycho-Analytic Therapy. *SE 11*.

Freud, S. (1912). Recommendations to Physicians Practising Psycho-Analysis. *SE 12*.

Freud, S. (1920). Beyond the Pleasure Principle. *SE 18*.

Freud, S. (1926). Inhibitions, Symptoms and Anxiety. *SE 20*.

Garland, C. (1998). Thinking about Trauma. In: C. Garland (Ed.), *Understanding Trauma: A Psychoanalytical Approach* (pp. 9–31). London: Duckworrth.

Gilligan, J. (2000). *Violence: Reflections on our Deadliest Epidemic*. London: Jessica Kingsley.

Glasser, M. (1984). Aggression and Sadism in the Perversions. In I. Rosen (Ed.), *Sexual Deviation* (pp. 279–300). Oxford University Press.

Gordon, J. & Whiteley, J.S. (1979). *Group Approaches in Psychiatry*. London: Routledge.

Gordon, J. (1999). Paula Heimann's Question and Group Analysis. *Psychoanal. Psychother. 13*: 107–116.

Gordon, J. (2004). Review of *Dangerous Patients: A Psychodynamic Approach to Risk Assessment and Management*. *Psychoanal. Psychother. 18*: 347–351.

Guttman, L.C. (1966). Order Analysis of Correlation Matrices. In R.B. Cattell (Ed.), *Handbook of Multivariate Experimental Psychology* (pp. 439–458). Chicago: Rand McNally.

Halton, W. (1994). Some Unconscious Aspects of Organizational Life: Contributions from Psychoanalysis. In: A. Obholzer & V. Roberts (Eds.), *The Unconscious at Work* (pp. 11–18). London: Routledge.

Heimann, P. (1950). On Counter-Transference. *Int. J. Psycho-Anal. 31*: 81–84.

Hinshelwood, R.D. (1979). The Community as Analyst. In: R.D. Hinshelwood & N. Manning (Eds.), *Therapeutic Communities: Reflections and Progress*. London: Routledge.

Hinshelwood, R.D. (1987a). The Psychotherapist's Role in a Large Psychiatric Institution. *Psychoanalytic Psychotherapy* 2: 207–215.

Hinshelwood, R.D. (1987b). *What Happens In Groups: Psychoanalysis, the Individual and the Community*. London: Free Asssociation Books.

Hinshelwood, R.D. (1989). Communication Flow in the Matrix. *Group Analysis* 22: 261–269.

Hinshelwood, R.D. (1992). Psychodynamic Formulation in Assessment for Psychotherapy. *British Journal of Psychotherapy 8*:166–174.

Hinshelwood, R.D. (1994). Attacks on the Reflective Space: Containing Primitive Emotional States. In: V.L. Schermer & M. Pines (Eds.), *Ring of Fire: Primitive Affects and Object Relationships in Group Psychotherapy*. London: Routledge.

Hinshelwood, R.D. (1997). *Therapy or Coercion*. London: Karnac.

Hinshelwood, R.D. (1998). Creatures of Each Other: Some Historical Considerations of Responsibility and Care and Some Present Undercurrents. In: A Foster and V.Z. Roberts (Eds.), *Managing Mental Health in the Community: Chaos and Containment*. London: Routledge.

Hinshelwood, R.D. (1999). The Difficult Patient: the Role of "Scientific Psychiatry" in Understanding Patients with Chronic Schizophrenia or Personality Disorder. *Brit. J. Psychiat. 174*: 187–190.

Hinshelwood. R.D. & Skogstad, W. (Eds.) (2000). *Observing Organisations: Anxiety, Defence and Culture in Health Care*. London: Taylor & Francis.

Hinshelwood, R.D. & Chiesa, M. (Eds.) (2001). *Organisations, Anxieties and Defences: Towards a Psychoanalytic Social Psychology*. London: Whurr.

Hinshelwood, R.D. (2001). *Thinking about Institutions*. London: Jessica Kingsley.

Hinshelwood, R.D. (2004). *Suffering Insanity: Psychoanalytic Essays on Psychosis*. London: Brunner-Routledge.

Hirschhorn, L. (1995). *The Workplace Within: Psychodynamics of Organizational Life*. Cambridge, Mass.: MIT Press.

Hochschild, A. (1983). *The Managed Heart: Commercialization of Human Feeling*. Berkeley: California University Press.

Hoffman, I. & Gill, M.M. (1988). A Scheme for Coding the Patient's Experience of the Relationship with the Therapist (PERT): Some Applications, Extensions and Comparisons. In: H. Dahl, H. Kächele & H. Thomä (Eds.), *Psychoanalytic Process Research Strategies*. Berlin: Springer.

Horowitz, M. (1991). *Personal Schemas and Maladaptive Interpersonal Behavior*. Chicago: University of Chicago Press.

Hughes, T. (1969). *Seneca's Oedipus*. London: Faber & Faber.

Hughes, T. (1999). *Aeschylus: The Oresteia*. London: Faber & Faber.

Jaques, E. (1955). Social Systems as a Defence Against Persecutory and Depressive Anxiety. In: M. Klein, P. Heimann & R. Money-Kyrle (Eds.), *New Directions in Psycho-Analysis*. London: Tavistock.

Joseph, B. (1989). *Psychic Equilibrium and Psychic Change: Selected Papers of Betty Joseph*. E.B. Spillius & M. Feldman (Eds.). London: Tavistock.

Kernberg, O.F. (1980). *Internal World and External Reality*. New York: Jason Aronson.

Kernberg, O.F. (1984). *Severe Personality Disorders: Psychotherapeutic Strategies*. New Haven, CT: Yale University Press.

Khan, M.R. (1963). The Concept of Cumulative Trauma. Reprinted in *The Privacy of the Self* (pp. 42–58). London: Hogarth, 1986.

Klein, M. (1946). Notes on Some Schizoid Mechanisms. In: *Envy and Gratitude and Other Works 1946–1963* (pp. 1–24). London: Hogarth.

Knowlson, J. (1997). *Damned to Fame: Life of Samuel Beckett*. London: Bloomsbury.

Koenigsberg, H.W., Kernberg, O.F., Stone, M.H., Appelbaum, A.H., Yeomans, FE., & Diamond, D. (2000). *Borderline Patients: Extending the Limits of Treatability*. New York: Basic Books.

Kreeger, L. (Ed.) (1975). *The Large Group: Dynamics and Therapy*. London: Constable.

Leary, T. (1957). *Interpersonal Diagnosis of Personality: A Functional Theory and Methodology for Personality Evaluation*. New York: Ronald Press.

Luborsky, L. & Crits-Christoph, P. (1990). *Understanding Transference*. New York: Basic Books.

Lucas, R. (2003). Risk Assessment in General Psychiatry: a Psychoanalytic Perspective. In: R. Doctor (Ed.), *Dangerous Patients: A Psychodynamic Approach to Risk Assessment and Management*. London: Karnac.

McCarthy, B. (1988). Are incest victims hated? *Psychoanal. Psychother. 3*: 113–120.

Main, T.F. (1975). Some Psychodynamics of Large Groups. In: L. Kreeger (Ed.), *The Large Group: Dynamics and Therapy*. London: Constable.

Main, T. (1989). *The Ailment and Other Psychoanalytic Essays*. London: Free Association Press.

Menzies Lyth, I. (1960). A Case Study in the Functioning of Social Systems as a Defence against Anxiety. *Human Relations 13*: 95–121.

Money-Kyrle, R. (1956). Normal Counter-Transference and Some of its Deviations. *Int. J. Psycho-Anal. 37*: 360–366.

Morgan, D. & Ruszczynski, S. (Eds.) (2007). *Lectures in Violence, Perversion and Delinquency*. London: Karnac.

Murray, H.A. (1938). *Explorations in Personality*. New York: Oxford University Press.

Newrith, C., Meux, C. & Taylor, P. (2006). *Personality Disorder and Serious Offending: Hospital Treatment Models*. London: Hodder Arnold.

Obholzer, A. & Roberts, V.Z. (1994). *The Unconscious at Work: Individual and Organizational Stress in the Human Services*. London: Routledge.

Ogden, T.H. (1980). On the Nature of Schizophrenic Conflict. *Int. J. Psycho-Anal. 61*: 513–533.

Ogden, T.H. (1983). The Concept of Internal Object Relations. *Int. J. Psycho-Anal. 64*: 227–241.

OPD Task Force (2001). *Operationalized Psychodynamic Diagnostics: Foundations and Manual*. Seattle, WA: Hogrefe & Huber.

Owens, B. (1956). It Don't Show on Me. *Stars Over Bakersfield*. Intermusic, CTS 55418.

Parker, M. (2006). *Dynamic Security*. London: Jessica Kingsley.

PDM Task Force (2006). *Psychodynamic Diagnostic Manual*. Silver Spring, MD: Alliance of Psychoanalytic Organizations.

Perelberg, R.J. (Ed.) (1999). *Psychoanalytic Understanding of Violence and Suicide*. London: Routledge.

Pfäfflin, F. & Adshead, G. (Eds.) (2004). *A Matter of Security*. London: Jessica Kingsley.

Pick, I. (1985). Working Through in the Countertransference. *Int. J. Psycho-Anal. 66*: 157–166.

Pilgrim, D. (1988). Psychotherapy in British Special Hospitals: a Case of Failure to Thrive. *Free Associations 11*: 58–72.

Pilgrim, D. (1997). *Psychotherapy and Society*. London: Sage.

Racker, H. (1968). *Transference and Countertransference*. London: Maresfield Reprints.

Robbins, M. (1993). *Experiences of Schizophrenia: An Integration of the Personal, Scientific and Therapeutic.* New York: The Guilford Press.

Rosenfeld, H. (1987). *Impasse and Interpretation.* London: Tavistock/ Routledge.

Sandler, J., Dare, C. & Holder, A. (1973). *The Patient and the Analyst: The Clinical Framework of Psychoanalysis.* London: Allen & Unwin.

Schaefer, E.S. (1965). Configuration Analysis of Children's Reports of Parent Behavior. *Journal of Consulting Psychology 29*: 552–557.

Schlapobersky, J. (1996). A Group Analytic Perspective: From the Speech of Hands to the Language of Words. In C. Cordess & M. Cox (Eds.), *Forensic Psychotherapy: Crime, Psychodynamics and the Offender Patient, Vol. 1: Mainly Theory* (pp. 227–244). London: Jessica Kinglsey.

Segal, H. (1977). Counter-transference. *Int. J. Psycho-Anal. Psychother. 6*: 31–37.

Segal, H. (1997). The uses and abuses of countertransference. In: J. Steiner (Ed.) *Psychoanalysis, Literature and War: Papers 1972–1995.* London: Routledge.

Shedler, J. & Westin, D. (2006). Personality Diagnosis with the Shedler-Westin Assessment Procedure (SWAP): Bridging the Gulf between Science and Practice. In: PDM Task Force (2006), *Psychodynamic Diagnostic Manual.* Silver Spring, MD: Alliance of Psychoanalytic Organizations.

Stanton, A.H. & Schwartz, M.S. (1954). *The Mental Hospital.* New York: Basic Books.

Steiner, J. (1993). *Psychic Retreats: Pathological Organizations in Psychotic, Neurotic and Borderline Patients.* London: Routledge.

Steiner, J. (2006). Interpretative Enactments and the Analytic Setting. *Int. J. Psycho-Anal. 87*: 315–320.

Stoller, R.J. (1975). *Perversion: the Erotic Form of Hatred.* London: Quartet.

Strupp, H. & Binder, J. (1984). *Psychotherapy in a New Key: A Guide to Time-Limited Dynamic Psychotherapy.* New York: Basic Books.

Sugarman, A. (1994). Trauma and Abuse: an Overview. In: *Victims of Abuse: The Emotional Impact of Child and Adult Trauma* (pp. 1–21). Madison, CT: International Universities Press.

Sullivan, H.S. (1953). *The Interpersonal Theory of Psychiatry.* New York: Norton.

Susskind, P. (1994). *Perfume.* London: Bloomsbury Classics.

Theodosius, C. (2006). Recovering Emotion from Emotion Management. *Sociology 40*: 893–910.

Turquet, P.M. (1975). Threats to Identity in the Large Group. In: L. Kreeger (Ed.), *The Large Group: Dynamics and Therapy*. London: Constable.

Webster, C.D., Douglas, K.S., Eaves, D. & Hart, S.D. (1997). *The HCR-20: Assessing the Risk for Violence. Version 2*. Lutz, FL: Psychological Assessment Resources, Inc.

Webster, C.D., Martin, M., Brink, J., Nicholls, T.L. & Middleton, C. (2004). *Short-Term Assessment of Risk and Treatability (START)*. Coquitlam, BC: BC Mental Health and Addiction Services.

Weiss, J. & Sampson, H. (1986). *The Psychoanalytic Process: Theory, Clinical Observation and Empirical Research*. New York: Guilford.

Welldon, E.V. (1984). Application of Group Analytic Psychotherapy to those with Sexual Perversions. In: T.E. Lear (Ed.), *Spheres of Group Analysis* (pp. 96–108). London: Group Analytic Society Publications.

Welldon, E.V. (1992). *Mother, Madonna, Whore: The Idealization and Denigration of Motherhood*. London: Karnac.

Welldon, E.V. (1993). Forensic Psychotherapy and Group Analysis. *Group Analysis 26*: 487–502.

Welldon, E.V. (1996). The Psychotherapist and Clinical Tutor. In: C. Cordess & M. Cox (Eds.), *Forensic Psychotherapy: Crime, Psychodynamics and the Offender Patient, Vol. II: Mainly Practice* (pp. 177–187). London: Jessica Kingsley.

Welldon, E.V. (1997). Let the Treatment Fit the Crime: Forensic Group Psychotherapy. *Group Analysis 30*: 9–26.

Wiggins, J.S. (1982). Circumplex Models of Interpersonal Behavior in Clinical Psychology. In P.C. Kendall & J.N. Butcher (Eds.), *Perspectives in Personality, Vol.1*. Greenwich, CT: JAI Press.

Winnicott, D.W. (1949). Hate in the Countertransference. *Int. J. Psycho-Anal. 30*: 69–74

Winnnicot, D.W. (1960). The Theory of the Parent-Infant Relationship. *Int. J. Psycho-Anal. 41*: 585–595.

INDEX

www.ingramcontent.com/pod-product-compliance
Ingram Content Group UK Ltd.
Pitfield, Milton Keynes, MK11 3LW, UK
UKHW022201190926
475702UK00003B/145
* 9 7 8 0 3 6 7 1 0 5 9 3 8 *